ISBN: 9781313542494

Published by:
HardPress Publishing
8345 NW 66TH ST #2561
MIAMI FL 33166-2626

Email: info@hardpress.net
Web: http://www.hardpress.net

QUAKER PIONEERS

IN

RUSSIA.

BY

JANE BENSON,

Author of " From the Lune to the Neva."

LONDON:

HEADLEY BROTHERS,

14, BISHOPSGATE STREET WITHOUT, E.C.

———

1902.

HEADLEY BROTHERS,

PRINTERS,

LONDON; AND ASHFORD, KENT.

Dedicated

TO THE MEMORY OF

MY FATHER AND MOTHER,

GEORGE AND ANNE EDMONDSON.

CONTENTS.

LIST OF ILLUSTRATIONS.

——

INTRODUCTION.

WE have in our possession a number of pictures, some lithographs, others coloured prints, which were bought in the city of Petersburg nearly eighty years ago. They used to be a source of great pleasure to a certain little child, especially when her father or mother could be induced to "talk about Russia," and add personal recollections to the suggestions of the pictures. They were, in fact, the child's first conscious connection with that vast country.

Her parents told her it was her native land, and they introduced to her by description some of its inhabitants. For instance, they spoke of Theodosia, the maid who was so often guilty of drinking out of the night-light glass the oil on which the little float depended for feeding its dim flame. It was a strange taste of the maid's the child thought, and it was a pity that, in order to gratify it, she took oil that was not her own.

They told her also of the frosty morning when the same girl had rushed screaming to her mistress declaring that the bed was on fire upstairs! The crackling and flashing of the electric sparks her own energetic parting of the bedclothes had induced, could be nothing less than real fire "she was sure."

She ought to be able to remember Theodosia her mother said, for before they left Okta the little one used sometimes to act as interpreter, giving in Russ to the maid in the kitchen a simple message entrusted to her in English in the parlour.

"Yes," her father would now and then add, "that was an opportunity lost. It would have been easy to keep up her Russ if she had not so persistently asserted on their voyage home that it was only the servants' language and was no longer needed, as the servants—represented to her mind by the sailors—all spoke English." The child had, or fancied she had, a dim recollection of this, but it has quite faded now.

More interesting than even Theodosia was the description of the man who so cheerfully took off his birch-bark boots and sold them to her father for a few kopeks that they might be sent to England as a specimen of the sort of foot-covering worn by the Russian peasants. One of the very boots* was often on the table before her and not only did it show that it had actually seen road service, but that the man had kept his promise of washing it in the brook if the price were doubled.

"What wilt thou do now?" was the question invariably waited for at this point by the young listener, to be followed by the wayfarer's astonishing reply to her father, "I saw plenty of birch-trees as I came along, I will sit down by the brook-side and make myself another pair!"

In this way was everything connected with Russia kept up in the child's mind, and as time went on and

---

* The other boot had been presented to a museum at Blackburn.

she became able to follow the sequence of events and
to appreciate the motives that lay beneath them so
far as human will was concerned, she was introduced
in the same manner to Daniel Wheeler's family and
encouraged to add to the interest of childhood the
esteem and admiration of later years. The obedience
to the call of duty and the perfect self-sacrifice with
which the whole family followed where duty led,
whether to Okta, to Volkovo, or in the end to sad
Shoosharry were never lost sight of.

Similarly her father kept before her mind his
abiding consciousness of the advantage it had been to
himself to be associated, while yet a youth, with so
genial, even humorous, a man and at the same time
one of such deep spiritual experience as Daniel
Wheeler.

Years still passed steadily and swiftly along and the
pictures and the child were growing old together,
when one May morning in 1895 the usual issue of
The Friend contained two Shoosharry sketches
which stirred her dormant memories once more. One
was a side view of the dwelling house of the Wheeler
family, the other a sketch of two graves in the burial-
ground at Shoosharry which was given to the Society
of Friends by the Emperor Nicholas of that day.
The former, it was said, was likely soon to be
demolished to make room for "extensive re-building,"
the latter remain as a touching memento of Daniel
Wheeler's wife and younger daughter, the darling
Janingka.

Not immediately, but suddenly one later day it
came into the *child's* mind that there were scenes in
that Russian life of which she believed herself to be

the last remaining record-keeper, and it occurred to her that it would be well for her to look over her treasured bundle of old letters again, and try to put the records into some kind of order for the benefit of whomsoever they might interest in time to come.

The carrying out of this thought has proved a pleasant resource for an invalid during the past year, and the following pages are the result.

Many letters not fully investigated before have been re-read and made use of, while the few conversations here reported are given in the words used in telling them to herself in the days of her youth, as nearly as she can remember them.

In short, this is just a simple narrative of scenes which really took place in connection with an experiment that she believes to have been unique.

One more remark is due. The present title was used by a relative not long ago for a lecture referring to the same subject, and he included other names among the Pioneers in addition to those originally thought of. His Cousin wishes to thank him for the permission to use both title and extension idea which she gladly and gratefully accepts.

J. B.

Southport.
    May, 1902.

I.

ALLEN AND GRELLET.

WE do not propose to offer here anything even approaching a condensed biography of these two remarkable Friends ; that has been already well and exhaustively written in certain interesting volumes which are still to be found on the bookshelves of the present Quaker generation. They are perhaps not quite so much read as they used to be, which is a misfortune for the readers.

Our object in this chapter is merely to draw from those volumes the thread which connects the two Friends with the Emperor Alexander, and thus to make good our claim for their position of Pioneers.

It is pretty generally known amongst us that Etienne de Grellet was a member of one of the noble families of France which suffered so severely during the " great revolutionary struggle " which swept over that country at the end of the 18th century. Having been born in the year 1773 he had arrived at early manhood before the circumstances of his family made it desirable for him and his brother Joseph to absent themselves from France. They spent a short time in Demerara but eventually found themselves in New York. In their state of uncertainty as to the welfare of their parents as well as to the prospects for their own means of livelihood, they decided to retire to Long Island "where they could live more privately and agreeably, and they settled down for the summer at Newtown."

When taking their last leave of their father he had given them a parting maxim—always to choose the company of their seniors in age and their superiors in rank and abilities, in preference to their inferiors. In accordance with that advice they had made acquaintance with the family of Colonel Corsa who, in addition to his good standing in society, possessed a daughter who was able to speak French. This, considering that the brothers were perfectly ignorant of the English language on their arrival, was an additional inducement to visit at the Colonel's house. It was to be of greater importance to Stephen than he dreamed of.

One day the conversation there turned upon William Penn ; and the daughter saying that she had his works and would lend them to him, Stephen's curiosity was excited. "He had heard of him as a statesman and politician and expected to find something relating to these subjects in his books. He took the volume, a large folio, to his lodgings and, with the help of a dictionary, began to translate it. The subject which first engaged his attention, however, was of so different a nature from what he had anticipated that he soon laid it aside without proceeding far in the attempt to make out its contents."

It was some time before he made a second attempt at the translation and in that interval a great change had taken place in himself. The Divine Spirit had in a remarkable manner spoken directly to his own, and as he now happily yielded himself implicitly to the moulding power of the new influence "the objects and pursuits of his life were completely and permanently changed."

He took up "No Cross No Crown" again, and the amount of his perseverance in studying it will be better realised if we remember that he had to refer to his dictionary for the meaning of nearly every word.

He read it twice through and then turned to the translation of an English Bible by the same slow process.

It was at this time that Stephen and his brother heard one evening at Colonel Corsa's that a meeting for divine worship was to be held next day in the Friends' Meeting House, by two Englishwomen on a religious visit to America, to which they two were invited. "We felt inclined to go," he says. The Friends were Deborah Darby and Rebecca Young.

But we will not pursue our extracts further at this point ; the details of Stephen Grellet's preparation for the peculiar missionary work in which his future life was to be mostly employed, will be found in the volumes already alluded to.

He was then in his 22nd year, yet it is not until the year 1814, when he was aged nearly forty, that we find the first decided trace of the thread for which we are seeking.

In the intervening years he had been sent by his Divine Master hither and thither on the face of the earth on various errands. His service was an arduous one, for he was peculiarly fitted by his inheritance of polished manners and cultured speech to convey the Master's messages to the great ones of many lands.

In the early spring of 1814 he paid a second series of visits to meetings in England and Ireland, and just previous to that he had spent more than three quarters of a year on the European continent, which, we need scarcely say, was then immersed in the horrors of war, for the Allied Powers were struggling desperately to keep within bounds the man who intended to be the conqueror of the western world. Stephen Grellet had come in contact with soldiers by hundreds belonging to both parties of belligerents, and, if we except a few instances amongst the Cossacks, had been kindly received and well treated by all.

He came back to England with a heart full of sadness at the scenes he had witnessed, together with a longing to be sent to some of the rulers as an ambassador of peace.

Although he had been so great a traveller, and moreover had been a member of the Society of Friends in America for many years, this was only his second opportunity of attending the London Yearly Meeting, and he looked forward with exceeding interest to again uniting with English Friends in their annual assembly. With many of them he was already affectionately acquainted.

It was a time of great excitement in London generally.

Before the close of the Yearly Meeting sittings a rumour was heard that the King of Prussia, the Emperor of Russia, and some other Royalties then in Paris, would probably cross the channel to England.

This seeming to our Friend an answer to the prayer which had long been rising in his heart, he made his feelings known to the Yearly Meeting, at the same time suggesting that any action which might be decided on would have much greater weight if taken by the representative body of Friends now officially gathered together.

The value of the suggestion was fully acknowledged, but as the crowned heads alluded to " had not yet come to England and possibly might not come, it did not appear proper then to prepare any addresses to them, but by a suitable minute the Yearly Meeting directed the ' Meeting for Sufferings ' to act in it as soon as way should open to carry into effect this concern."

In due time the Royal guests did arrive, the Meeting for Sufferings obeyed the behest of the superior body, and a committee was formed to prepare the addresses already spoken of.

Stephen Grellet here writes in his diary : "Joseph Gurney Bevan took so much interest in it that after hearing the views of Friends respecting the subjects the addresses should embrace, he, though now blind and in great feebleness of body, nevertheless undertook to prepare these documents. He has a very clear head and above all a very pious and tender spirit."

We do not know if this was an unusual proceeding in those days, but whoever was initially answerable for their preparation, the two addresses were passed by the full committee. and signed on its behalf by " William Allen, clerk to the Meeting." This Friend whose name was, in after years, so intimately coupled

with that of his French comrade, now, for the first
time, takes a place by his side as a co-worker.

That he was, by nature and training, well fitted for
that position, the following brief summary of his
character will convince us. It is quoted from the
lecture already alluded to.

" A page from William Allen's diary at once gives
the impression of a man of great energy of character,
of high scientific attainments, of deep sympathy
for his fellows, of unswerving allegiance to duty, yet,
withal of courtly manners combined with great
business capacity."

The fact that William Allen's signature was appended to the two addresses may have led to his
being summoned by name to attend the Emperor at
the Pulteney Hotel to arrange for the official reception
of them. On the other hand he was already known
to several members of the English Royal family from
being associated with them in plans for the alleviation
of distress and the improvement of the condition
of the poor generally. Along with the Dukes of Kent
and Sussex he was especially interested in the subject
of education. The problem, which is still unsolved, of
how to provide free and suitable instruction for every
child in the kingdom was already claiming the attention of the thoughtful.

There was some little difficulty in getting the arrangement with the Emperor accomplished. William
Allen was desired to present himself at the Hotel at
9 o'clock on a certain Saturday evening. He was
punctual but the members of the Royal party were all
absent. He remained till between 12 and 1 o'clock,
then finding that Count Lieven's servants were

ordered home, he says, " I gave my card to one of them, desiring him to inform his master that I had waited till that time, and would do myself the pleasure of calling upon him at Harley Street the next morning."

The next was a " First-day " morning (6th mo. 19th) but William Allen was in Harley Street about a quarter before ten. Count Lieven was already out but expected home soon. W. A. decided to wait.

Shortly after eleven he was summoned to join the Count in his carriage at the door. The moment he was seated they drove rapidly away, and as they went his companion informed him that the Emperor wished to attend one of the Friends' meetings, and that there was no other time for it than the present.

Such a wish was, of course, a command. There were six different meetings in London, W. A. told the Count, and suggested attending one in the afternoon, but finding that nothing but the present moment could be entertained, he replied, " Then it is quite plain we must go to the nearest, which is Westminster, and lose no time otherwise it may be broken up." They therefore called for the Royal party on the way and proceeded to Westminster Meeting.

Can we adequately imagine the feeling of the meeting when William Allen showed the Emperor, the young Duke of Oldenburg, the King of Wurtemburg, and Count Lieven, the ambassador, to seats facing the meeting ? The Duchess of Oldenburg (the Emperor's sister) preferred the first form on the women's side. The Emperor and the whole party conducted themselves with the greatest seriousness.

The meeting remained in silence about a quarter of an hour, then, three of the ministers in the gallery had something given them to say, and we may fully agree with William Allen's remark that Friends were evidently "owned" at that meeting.

On returning to his carriage the Emperor fixed the next day but one for receiving the deputation, which was to consist only of William Allen and "the Friend who spoke second"—John Wilkinson.

Stephen Grellet was added later by permission, and no doubt communication of thought was made easier by the addition of his perfect French.

Among a number of old Russian papers we found one day a copy of an extract from a letter of "Margaret Fisher's," but without direction or other intimation for whose benefit it had been copied. Its date is 6th month 22, 1814 (the day after the Emperor fixed to receive the deputation) and it mentions that Stephen Grellet had paid their family a most animated visit the evening before, only a couple of hours after he had left the Grand Duchess and the Emperor. The latter had declined a formal deputation but desired an hour's quiet conversation, which Stephen Grellet thought had been appreciated by them all.

The questions the Emperor asked referred generally to the realities of everyday life : he liked our principles, he said, so far as he had heard them, but he had the wisdom to recognise the long distance that often exists between preaching and practice. He had previously remarked that he liked the meeting he attended and now he wanted to visit a Friend's house. He also inquired, "Why do not some of your people come to my country? If any do, don't make application to others, come immediately to me ; I promise you protection and every assistance in my power."

He took leave of his three visitors with more than kindness—with affection, expressing the hope that when far separated they would often remember each other. Stephen Grellet added, the letter goes on to say, that as they left the Emperor's presence they met the King of Prussia on the landing and had a few minutes conversation with him. They spoke of the blessings of peace, to which Frederick William characteristically replied, "I wish peace with all the world, but it is necessary to have war in order to attain peace."

In compliance with the Emperor's wish an arrangement was made for a Brighton Friend—John Glaisyer—to receive a call from him as he returned from Portsmouth, but the crowd in the street was so great that his carriage could not approach the door of the house.

It was a great disappointment to all parties at the time, but the manner in which Alexander managed for himself later to obtain an interview with a Friend's family in their own house, was infinitely better than any pre-arranged visit could have been.

As he and his party were on their journey to Dover when they returned to the Continent, they noticed two Friends—Nathaniel Rickman and his wife— standing at the door of a house at a little distance from the road. The Emperor stopped his carriage, got out, and courteously inquired of them if they belonged to the people commonly called Quakers.

On receiving a reply in the affirmative he next asked leave for himself and sister to enter the house, which of course was granted. They stayed some time, looking over it, taking refreshment, and telling their host and hostess, to whom it was news, of their attending a meeting, and their interviews with members of the Society, in London. Here his favourable opinion of Friends was confirmed—the farm and the house were well cared for and orderly, and he did not forget his impressions when the time came for making use of them.

II.

DANIEL WHEELER AND HIS ASSISTANT.

WHEN the Emperor Alexander came to the end of his visit in our little island and bade farewell to the friends he had made here, there is no doubt that he intended they should hear from him without delay on his return to Russia. But he could not foresee the unwelcome re-appearance of that troublesome exile Napoleon, and though his second grasp of power was a short one, its consequences were sufficiently far-reaching to account for the Emperor's three years silence.

It would be a great mistake, however, to suppose that because plans are not perceptibly progressing they are not making progress at all. In this instance the work of preparation was certainly being carried on in a very remarkable manner, so that, when the time arrived for Alexander's thoughts to revert to his home affairs and the impressions he had received in England, the man who was to help him in the work he wished at once to set about, was ready and silently waiting for his call.

In the early part of the year 1817 the call was heard. Our old acquaintance, Count Lieven, the Russian ambassador, received an intimation of the Emperor's desire to bring into cultivation, as speedily

as possible, the waste crown lands around the city of
Petersburg, and the Count was requested to make an
inquiry for a suitable person to superintend the work.
He must be an Englishman and a member of the
Society of Friends.

The wishes of the Emperor were made known
throughout the meetings of that Society and a quick
response came from Sheffield.

Daniel Wheeler, one of the recorded Ministers of
that meeting, informed his fellow members that a
prospect of foreign service had been resting in his
mind for the last two or three years ; moreover that
his Lord and Master had lately shown him that Russia
was the country to which he must look.   Therefore,
as he was made willing to go wherever he was sent,
he offered himself for the situation at Petersburg.

His friends could only regretfully confess that he
was especially well qualified for the position to be
filled, and pass on his offer, which was gladly accepted
by the Emperor.

Daniel Wheeler, like Stephen Grellet, was a convinced Friend.   From a fragment of autobiography
that he felt it his duty to write in his sixty-first year,
we learn that he was born in 1771, and that, from his
twelfth year, when he lost his widowed mother, until
he was nearly twenty-five, his life had been a rugged
one.   Part of the time engaged in the navy, the last
four years in the army, he had experienced to the full
extent the hardships inseparable from both services,
and he had neither escaped their temptations nor yet
passed scatheless through them.

When he was about twenty-five years old his
regiment was ordered to the West Indies under Sir

DANIEL WHEELER.

Ralph Abercrombie and it was during the voyage out, in the midst of a severe storm, that his conscience was finally awakened to the consequences of his unsteady life.

" He took counsel of no one." He afterwards said of himself, " No human means were made use of—it was altogether the immediate work of the Holy Spirit on my heart." Submitting to the guidance and discipline of that Spirit, he soon felt his profession to be out of keeping with the command " Love your enemies" and " Do good to them that hate you," which are the burden of the New Testament. Therefore on his return to England he gave up his commission in the army and betook himself to Sheffield, where his eldest sister had been living for some time. She had married a " Quaker " there, changing her name from Wheeler to Hoyland.

Finding, as he learned more of their views, that they were nearer to his ideal than any he had yet met with, he sought admission to the Society, and soon followed his sister's example by marrying one of their members—Jane, daughter of Thomas and Rachel Brady, of Thorne.

" He had already opened a shop in the seed trade," a correspondent says, " and, after acquiring the first reputation in Sheffield as a tradesman, he took a farm, as if to give proof of his practical skill in agriculture. His farm excited the admiration of the neighbourhood, and demonstrated that his talents in this direction too were of a superior kind."

Thus when the Emperor's inquiry reached Sheffield the desired manager was ready. To his surprise and unbounded relief his wife was also ready;

Ruth's language to Naomi rose to her lips, and she encouraged him to make any sacrifice for the sake of duty.

It was concluded that Daniel Wheeler should, in the first instance, visit Petersburg alone, that he might look round and gain some idea of the land to be under his care, and that the Emperor might, at the same time, make acquaintance with him—the man whose faith was bringing not only himself but his whole family to an unknown country. Their mutual confidence was never shaken.

Daniel Wheeler spent more than a month at Petersburg, was introduced to the Emperor, and visited him at his Summer·Palace situated on the island of Kamenoi-Ostrov, one of the "picturesque group surrounded by the clear blue waters of the Neva." In returning from that visit he says, "We passed the hut that Peter the Great at one time inhabited; and we saw the boat built by his own hands. We passed through the public gardens which are beautiful."

As the result of his observations of the city and neighbourhood he writes, "I think the generality of the soil is better than I expected to see. I recognised clover and several kinds of grasses by the road side, and abundance of weeds in the gardens, of pretty much the same varieties that we have in England." During the ensuing winter Daniel Wheeler was actively engaged in winding up his affairs preparatory to leaving England, as well as in carrying out the commission of the Emperor to make ample provision of agricultural implements, seeds and cattle for his future use.

But there was another consideration more important still. He had a family of four sons and two daughters, for whose further education the arrangements presented considerable difficulty. But he had promised that he would take his entire family with him, and he meant to keep his word.

William Singleton, a Friend who had been reading master at Ackworth School when Joseph Donbavand was writing-master there, had taken an old residence (situated in what was then a suburb of Sheffield) and opened it as a boarding school for boys. He was induced to take this step by the offer of a few of his friends to guarantee him £200 a year if he would do so. But the school at Broomhall increased so rapidly that they were not called upon for the money.

"William Singleton's pupils idolized him," one of them has written. Two of Daniel Wheeler's sons were of their number; the eldest had left and would be able to help his father, but three sons and the two daughters were still needing instruction.

Feeling a want of human sympathy and counsel, their father thought he could scarcely ask them of a more suitable man than the one to whom he had entrusted his sons' education. So he walked up to Broomhall one fine evening and laid his wants before him.

"Thou must take a teacher with thee, Daniel, there is no question as to that," was William Singleton's first and very natural comment.

"Just so," replied his visitor, "that seems the only plan for securing that the children shall not suffer; but where shall I find him? We shall have difficulties to contend with, and we shall be like a city set on a hill, and in addition to these considerations the man

I want should be able to do something more than give book lessons—he must know how to use his hands, and such a man is not met with every day. However I cannot lose faith that I shall be helped in *all* things, the path has been made so clear before me thus far." "And will be still, Daniel. The man is waiting for thee, I think, as thou wast waiting for the Emperor," came in prompt reply, when William Singleton had heard the kind of man his friend had in his mind.

"Thou hast frequently met with my apprentice George Edmondson?" he continued.

"Yes, but he is very young!" was Daniel Wheeler's involuntary exclamation.

"He is very steady and I think combines all the qualities thou art looking for. As to himself, it will be of untold good to him to be under thy care. If the idea commends itself to thee as it rests in thy mind, I will give him the remainder of his apprenticeship, so satisfied am I that he is the helper thou needs."

Daniel Wheeler had been sure of sympathy from his friend, but this unhesitating offer of help took him by surprise. It was truly a startling answer to his faith and he went home comforted, for, as "the idea rested in his mind," he felt increasing unity with it.

The young man himself does not appear to have been consulted in the matter. It was the custom at that period for young people to be managed, not consulted, and they were expected to be obedient to what their elders thought best for them.

But in this instance, judging by a letter from George to one of his brothers, which has come to our hands along with more important papers, he would at once

have agreed to the arrangement if he *had* been asked.
And that is a satisfactory thought.

The letter was written at Broomhall in 1817, and
was simply a comment on his eldest brother's remark
that "Russia was too cold a country for Englishmen,"
to which he replied, in effect, that " if Frenchmen
could stand it Englishmen certainly could," with
sundry wise additions that are rather amusing from
the youngest of the three brothers. It was written
during Daniel Wheeler's preliminary absence in
Russia, before it was finally decided that even *he*
should try the Russian climate, therefore before any
inkling of his own good fortune—if I may use the
expression—could possibly have reached the youth.

Good fortune it certainly was. To go abroad under
the care of such a man as Daniel Wheeler was in
itself a privilege—to go abroad at all was out of the
reach of most people in 1817.

But there was one little cloud that overshadowed
George's natural gratification at having been selected
for this post, and in order to explain it we must go
back a few years to the time when William Singleton
was, as we have said, reading-master at Ackworth, and
his present apprentice was one of the scholars.

As a married master with a family, the reading-
master was provided with a house in the village of
Ackworth, and, finding one day that he should be
detained at the school later than usual, he decided to
send a message to his wife informing her of the
change. Looking round for a messenger, he noticed
a little curly headed boy of twelve who had not been
very long at the school, and calling him to his side,
said, " I want thee to take a message from me to my

wife, George,"—little dreaming of the consequences
that were to result from that message.

George felt very important and very happy, he was
going as a trusted messenger for the master he liked
best, and he was going out of bounds. He repeated
his message aloud to keep it in his memory.

His knock at the cottage door was answered by a
fair blue-eyed little maiden a year or two younger
than himself. She smiled but did not speak. He
delivered his message and she, still silent to him, went
to the foot of the stairs and called " Mother." It was
the first word she had spoken, the only word he
heard her speak while he remained at Ackworth, but
it was sufficient.

Her voice was so sweet, her manner so modest,
—in fact he made up his precocious mind that if ever
he had a wife she was to be the one. Of course he
did not confess this until long afterwards, but
"Mother" sounded in his ears all the way back to
school, and he thought if he could only listen to those
tones when he became a man, life would be full of
charm and beauty. When his boyhood's secret *did*
eventually leak out it explained a phase which had
been a mystery to his family. He had seemed to
them unaccountably, almost culpably, fastidious as to
the next step in his career, and it was not until the
news reached them of William Singleton's removal
to Broomhall, that any proposition as to his future
met with George's hearty co-operation, but from
that time he took the initiative himself. He obtained
his parents' leave to write to his old master and
inquire if he was likely to want an apprentice—to
which the fact of his present residence at Broomhall
in that capacity at once supplies the answer.

George's master was not so unobservant as his wife seemed on one occasion to fear; he was quite aware of the romance so quietly being acted in his own household and his only objection to it was the youth of the actors. "They did not know their own minds."

He imparted as much as he knew himself to his esteemed visitor and they both agreed that it only confirmed the suitability of their plan.

After reading this little episode it will not be difficult to imagine the cause of the one small cloud alluded to on George's horizon—he would no longer reside under the same roof as the owner of the magic voice.

He had the satisfaction of a quiet talk with her father and mother, which ended in something of an understanding being allowed between the young people, although neither engagement nor correspondence could be permitted.

But George felt that in his old master he had a friend at court, and said to himself, " Patience."

III.

THE DEPARTURE FOR RUSSIA.

THE party for Russia being now completed by the engagement of two labourers with their families, Daniel Wheeler and his little company set sail from Hull on the 22nd of June, 1818, in the ship *Arethusa* under the command of " pleasant and genial Captain Wharton." " She has proved herself a noble vessel," Daniel Wheeler writes on the 26th from the Elsinore Roads to a Friend in Sheffield, " and although much weighted on her decks with water-casks and cattle, she has borne her costly freight (to me not only costly but precious indeed) nearly 700 miles in this short time without any leakage, though sorely buffeted by wind and sea. . . . We were so amply supplied with every article of provision that our Hull friends could think of or prepare, that our fare has been very different from what is usual at sea." And Daniel Wheeler's opinion was that of an experienced man on all these points.

Perhaps a younger correspondent may be forgiven for specifying with regard to these provisions that the gooseberry pies and the green gooseberries (from which to make further supplies), so bountifully furnished by their English friends, had lasted until they were in a position to test the Danish fruit. This, they decided, was smaller than the English but of superior flavour. How much of the superior flavour was due to the difference between fruit freshly gathered and that a week old was a question that apparently did not occur to them.

Their creature comforts had indeed been so well attended to by their friends that neither delays from absence of wind to fill the sails, nor a whole week's detention later at Cronstadt, seems to have been considered a misfortune. "*After the first few days* the voyage had been thoroughly enjoyed."

The letter in which George Edmondson tells his family this is almost too ragged to be decipherable. It was the first they had received from him after the actual arrival of the party at their destination, and it bears the mark, we can imagine, of the many unfoldings and re-foldings it has undergone.

"On July the 8th," he says, "the guardship's boat boarded us and we had our first near view of the Russians." The evening before, as the party were on deck admiring a glorious sunset, they were startled by the boom of the Admiral's sunset gun—the fort's Good Night to the departing luminary just as he dips below the horizon.

They had had a quick passage of only sixteen days, but now they would have to rest idly a while at Cronstadt—the *Arethusa* could go no further. The depth of water in the Neva was variable and often insufficient for large vessels, in which case the transit of goods from this port to the city frequently took as long as the rest of the voyage. However, as we know, our travellers had good accommodation on board and they remained in their own quarters. There was abundance to interest them.

The Emperor Alexander and the King of Prussia were together once again, and the King's visit was being made the occasion of more military display in his honour than was the ordinary habit of the Russian court.

He and the Emperor were expected at Cronstadt the following day, they were told, but Alexander always avoided a crowd when possible, and the two monarchs appeared suddenly at a point considerably distant from the one at which they were expected. Yet nobody was disconcerted, it was too common an occurrence.

A boat with twenty rowers was waiting for them, they soon took their seats under its awning and proceeded to inspect the fleet which lay at anchor, outside. As they passed out of the harbour they were saluted by all the cannon with which it was surrounded, and as they approached the fleet they were again saluted by its combined artillery.

" This was a new scene to most of us," George naïvely wrote home, " and we had a fine opportunity of watching the manœuvres from the mast-head, as we were just in the midst of the firing."

To Daniel Wheeler, of course, all this was no novelty ;—probably it recalled scenes he would have preferred to forget, but the young teacher's years did not number twenty and everything was new to him. We do not hear that he was blamed by his chief, who was a man of wisdom and had learned to wait.

At length everything was ready for our party to leave the vessel, and they were transferred to a large boat with twelve oars for the passage to the city. They hoped to reach their new home the same evening, but the current of the Neva was against them ; they were nine hours on the water and did not land until eleven o'clock—too late to continue their journey that night. They therefore sent on the two men with their families and goods by the " lighter " to Okta and themselves stayed at an inn.

George writes, " At supper we had Russian waiters for the first time, and felt the inconvenience of not being able to speak the language, but by signs and a few words we had got hold of we managed very well."

The next afternoon they drove the mile and a half to their new home and found that, even in the midst of his regal hospitalities, Alexander had not forgotten his protegés.

The house prepared for them belonged to Count Bezborodka and was situated on the further bank of the Neva nearly opposite the Smolney Monastery. It was so near the village of Okta that it was generally included in it, being known by the same name. It was an excellent stuccoed brick house containing twenty-four rooms with the necessary stabling and outbuildings. There was a high wall round the yard to keep out the wolves at night. The whole was placed at Daniel Wheeler's disposal with orders that everything he required from the vessels was to be landed duty free, and whatever was deficient in the house was to be supplied according to his wishes.

The kind consideration of their Imperial master never failed them during their stay in his empire.

According to the custom of the country the two men and their families were accommodated in the lower part, the kitchens also were on the ground floor ; a room was set apart there for " meeting " and Daniel

Wheeler and his family occupied the twelve rooms of
the upper story.   To an English mind this does not
seem a satisfactory arrangement for several reasons,
and when the families to be accommodated on the
lower floor happened to be Russian instead of English
the consequences were even less easy to put up with.

But the family who had thus left their country at
the call of duty were not likely to place their own
pleasure and convenience first on the list of their
requirements.

Beds and necessary furniture of that kind had
been provided for them, which was fortunate, as they
arrived before the lighter which was bringing, not
only the men with their belongings in active and still
life, but the household goods that the Wheeler family
had brought from England too.

We are told, however, that again they found abundance to interest them while they were waiting.
"The Neva at this point is about half a mile broad
and the number of barks or rafts that float past every
day to the city is incredible.   They are laden with
hemp, tallow and provisions from noblemen's estates
in the interior and brought down by the current of
the river.   The uninterrupted waterway, 2,000 miles
long from the south-east corner of Russia-in-Europe
to the capital, is of immense value in opening up the
interior of the country and providing cheap carriage
for goods.

"When the cargoes are disposed of, the men who
bring them sell the rafts, which are made of deal,
for firewood or other purposes and return with the
proceeds, on foot to their owners, of whom men as
well as barks are the absolute property."

A ONE-SEATED DROSCHKY.

When their own boat arrived the next day, every-one was eager to unload and arrange the dear familiar objects so pleasant once more to see around them. Amongst these was a fine old-fashioned eight-day clock which was set up in a corner of the common sitting-room. They thought it would be particularly useful to have a trustworthy timepiece for general reference, but a use was made of it that never entered into their calculations.

In every Russian dwelling, the poorest as well as the most sumptuous, there may be seen facing you as you enter the hall, or the "living-room," the *Ikon*, a sort of square metal picture representing a saint, or some occurrence in the life of one, often by figures that seem to us very grotesque. These images vary in size, material and finish ; the cheapest are not more than an inch or two square, the more costly reaching the size of one or two feet. All orthodox members of the Greek church on entering the apartment bow towards the image and cross themselves before speaking to the master or mistress of the house. On looking around for the usual object of momentary worship in Daniel Wheeler's room, his visitors could find nothing so nearly resembling it as the "Grandfather's clock" and without attending to the protest of its owner they continued so to regard it. Thus early they learned that "in all that regards externals" the Russian peasant "is decidedly religious."

It is noticeable that Daniel Wheeler does not seem to have been called upon in Russia to preach publicly the gospel of Christ. His office there was, appar-ently, to give quietly to seeking hearts, here a message and there a message, as way opened, and with regard to the general public, to preach by example religion recognised as the spring of daily action in human life.

Two or three weeks elapsed and every day household affairs became more settled; Russian stoves and other conveniences were better understood and appreciated, and our friends felt themselves at liberty to begin their special work out of doors. They were indeed very anxious to begin it, for the summer was rapidly running its course; they were near the end of July, and in October possibly, though not certainly, they might be driven indoors by the hardening frost. They had, of course, examined the land so far as it could be done by themselves, and the report was that it was not so boggy as they expected from the accounts which had reached them in England. It was rather spongy than boggy being covered with a white moss to the depth, on an average, of about sixteen inches, with cowberry and other pretty bog plants, small shrubs and young fir trees, not tall but seriously interfering with their lines in surveying.

In poking about amongst this they discovered that beneath the foot and a half of sphagnum there were the roots of an old forest and occasionally near the surface some large tree trunks in an advanced stage of decay which would effectually prevent the use of a plough. Opinions were divided as to the time when, and the purpose for which, the forest had been destroyed. A part of a bomb-shell and a Swedish axe found during these operations led some of them to suppose it was destroyed in the wars between Charles XII. of Sweden and Peter the Great; others thought it more likely that the trees had been felled to furnish timber for the building of the city ;—the "window" Peter wisely felt was wanted to look out of into Europe.

One of the workers, less imaginative if more practical than the rest, sagely remarked, "In whatever manner and for whatever purpose the trees were removed, it seems to me it is *we* who have the *roots* to contend with, and at the very present time." Whereupon they returned to their plans.

It was evident that the first thing to do was to get rid of the superabundant water. To accomplish this they proposed to carry all round the boundary a wide, deep drain would have a good fall into the river Okta, and would serve for a fence as well as for a general outlet. (Wolves must be taken into consideration in preparing for the future.) Next they would intersect their plot with smaller drains, cutting it up into fields of about eight acres each— small fields, but their land was almost level and the drains must be close accordingly, while a continued connection between them and the main one must be carefully maintained throughout. By these means the surface would become sufficiently dry to proceed with other operations. At present it was one wide sop, the moss retaining the moisture like a sponge. Hacking up the moss would be the next step and then the disinterring of the tree roots. These would all be allowed to remain until the following season to dry and shrink that they might be lighter to carry off.

Some powder magazines being situated not far away it was forbidden to burn rubbish on the land.

Therefore, when dry, the roots from each field must be laid in a row down the middle, with the moss placed tidily on each side of them.

It was all well thought out, but where were the hands to carry the thought into execution? This small plot of 1,000 acres on which they were to try their "'prentice hands" seemed likely, with its buried roots and its miniature fir trees, to require an immense amount of manual labour.

Eighty years ago serfdom was universal on the large estates in Russia. The men and the land remained, or changed owners together. In many cases the serfs were allowed, or perhaps compelled, to hire themselves out according to their various abilities, the master receiving a percentage of their earnings, or a fixed sum for permission to work for themselves. Daniel Wheeler had engaged twenty-seven of these serfs from the estates around Okta to assist in the preliminary investigations, but they were scarcely more than sufficient for the daily tasks.

General D'junkovsky, who had charge of the public buildings of the city, had been commissioned by the Emperor to "look after the English farmers," and exceedingly kind and helpful they always found him. Through him government had promised them a large number of soldiers for the work, but they had not arrived. Our friends did not expect that these would prove to be soldiers of the fighting class, but probably road-makers and pioneers, such as are always required to accompany an army, and wished they would make their appearance.

The General had sent instructions to Okta as to the preparations to be made for the three to five hundred

men that were expected, which relieved Daniel
Wheeler of much anxiety ; for he certainly would not
have provided, of his own accord, anything like the
poor accommodation the General assured him was
sufficient.

He was ordered to prepare long shelves, six feet
wide, against the wall of a wooden building, to serve
as beds ; here they would sleep, in their clothes, side
by side. Their dining-table was a plank upon trestles
—the black bread and onions of their usual mid-day
meal needed no dishes, indeed, it seemed at first
sight that they might have called a table a luxury and
dispensed with it altogether, but it proved useful for
holding, at intervals of a few feet, the little heaps of
salt that they shook out of a curious bottle-like recep-
tacle made of the inner bark of the birch. They were to
be paid thirty kopeks, or about threepence a day, in
money ; clothes and food being found by the Emperor.

An interpreter had been sent to reside with the
English family, as they decided, considering the
pressure of out-door work, to leave the study of the
language until the short dark days of winter. A
Russian surveyor was also sent to assist them, but
when he was directed to take a level he was obliged to
confess his ignorance—he had never done such a thing !

One of the good rules for self-discipline, for which
George had to thank his old master, Wm. Singleton,
was to lose no opportunity of adding to his knowledge
—whether in his own line or not did not signify,—
knowledge of any kind was sure to be useful some
time. When George took up his abode at Broomhall,
a friend of his from their native town had already
been nearly a year in a land-surveyor's office in

Sheffield. Here was a good opportunity for putting the above advice into practice, and both his friend's master and his own being kindly disposed, by their permission and encouragement the young surveyor passed on to George the lessons in map and plan-drawing he received in the office, and in the practical work of surveying, whenever there was an afternoon to spare. He received in return literary instruction of one kind or another that we have no doubt often proved as useful to him as the power to survey a plot of land and draw a plan of it when measured proved on this occasion to the young tutor.

George now showed that he knew "how to use his hands," and, with the assistance of Daniel Wheeler's eldest son William, dispensed with the professional surveyor's services for the future, and had the plans for draining ready long before the men were there who were to be guided by them.

For some things it might be pleasant and comfortable to farm on this easy-going ask-and-have system, with no anxiety as to whether it would pay or not, but to men whose honest desire was to *make* it pay, the dilatory style of transacting business around them was very painful. The long wished for soldiers came at last, however, and were apparently comfortable in their quarters—or at least apathetic.

As soon as the frost took possession of the ground each winter these men returned to their headquarters, and our friends had no further responsibility concerning them until returning Spring again unlocked the workshop door and their services were once more needed.

IV.

OKTA AND WELCOME GUESTS.

NO delay that our friends could prevent was allowed on the morning after the soldiers' arrival, we may be sure. Although the site of the ancient forest was a mile and a half distant from the house, William and George met their men on the ground at five o'clock. A sufficient length to make a beginning was already marked out, and the young surveyors arranged their men, each man armed with a spade, at equal distances on the line of the proposed boundary drain. It looked a formidable array of workers.

When the signal was given to begin, the young masters were startled and impressed by the preliminary movements, as by one impulse these peasants, dirty, bearded and loosely garmented, removed their caps, crossed themselves devoutly and prayed in a few words—which were afterwards interpreted—to the Virgin Mary to intercede for a blessing on the work begun that day. The same desire, with variations, had been in their own hearts and notwithstanding the errors and superstition, they could not help feeling a sympathy with these rough specimens of humanity whose language they did not understand.

And yet, promising as was this entrance on the work, it was by very slow degrees that the drains were cut and the moss gathered off the land.

English energy was disgusted and despairing. The unusual power of " patient endurance," and of " dogged passive resistance " with which the Russian peasant is generally credited, was, no doubt, at times, useful to the poor serfs as a defence from the rapacity of their owners, but it also formed a barrier against the honest desire of conscientious employers to finish their work in proper time.

After long consideration Daniel Wheeler decided to try another plan with the men ; he had tried appealing to their sense of duty, he would now appeal to their self-interest.

He had them assembled, and told them through the interpreter that " their father the Emperor " had ordered him to give them threepence a day, and he had obeyed his orders.   But that, in the country he came from, people only expected three-pennyworth of work for threepence ; and he proposed to measure off a certain quantity of work that he considered worth the money, and when they had done it, they might go for the day ; or, if they wished to earn a little more, whatever they did after that should be measured at night and paid for at the same rate.

The men were astonished at the address, but the work went on more briskly next morning when the plan was tried.   The greater number left, however, when the allotted piece was done ; some because they were too idle to work, others because they did not believe the promises.   A few continued to dig, and at night their work was carefully measured and of course paid for to the full value. As they went away delighted with their extra gains, and surveying the money actually in their hands, they remarked with surprise one to another, " Why, this man does as he says he will ! " An instructive comment on the usual style of treating them.

The plan was kept up and had a marked effect upon the work, but this small experience gave our English friends an idea of the manner in which the ruler of such a people could be quietly and passively thwarted in his best endeavours for the general good.

Much curiosity was excited about this scheme of the Emperor's, and the strange people that he had brought into the country, but his favour secured them from annoyance at first, and very soon they were better known and appreciated for their own sakes. They had numerous visitors, and amongst them were many from the court.

George wrote home in November of 1818 that he had been very much surprised to see in an English newspaper the following paragraph :—

" The operations of the Quaker, Daniel Wheeler, to dig turf and drain the marshes of the Russian Metropolis, have begun with success. Last Wednesday his Excellency the Minister of the Interior viewed the manner of proceeding, which he greatly approved. It is hoped that the turf or peat thus procured will cause a considerable saving of wood and tend to the preservation of the forests." How the information had been transmitted was a mystery but he adds, " It was quite true (except that it was not *last* Wednesday) the Minister did come and seemed very much pleased with the work. William and I had been busy dragging the chain and clearing away obstructions, and you can imagine the state of our hands, when a carriage stopped and its occupant alighted and approached us. Of course we should never have dreamed of offering to shake hands, in whatever state they were, but he insisted on it with great warmth and cordiality."

Unfortunately he could not speak English, but he managed to express his good-will by this pleasant action. He had paid the visit at the Emperor's request, as Alexander was preparing to attend an important congress, and was greatly disappointed that first his Prussian guest and now the congress obliged him to postpone his personal visit to Daniel Wheeler's family for a longer time since their arrival than accorded either with his sense of politeness or his real inclination.

We find these foreign letters of ours sometimes give their little histories as if they had just happened, when perhaps we know quite well from other sources that months must have elapsed since they occurred. It was not until 1819 that George writes to a relative an account of the Emperor's first visit to them, but we know that it was really paid before the end of the previous summer. It had evidently been a very gratifying one. The letter says, "He came in so simple a style that no one could have taken him for an Emperor. It was in a small carriage drawn by only two horses, with no other attendant than the coachman he had with him in England. He proposed to look round at the work, and Daniel Wheeler said he would accompany him in his own droschky which was in readiness—that is a small low carriage used here, sometimes having one seat

The Emperor Alexander doing a kindly act on his way to visit Daniel Wheeler.

sometimes two. 'But you can go with me,' replied
Alexander, 'my carriage has two seats.'" And they
drove off together—the Quaker in his broad-brimmed
hat and the Monarch in full regimental costume.
They had tea on their return from the inspection, and
altogether the guest stayed about three hours. "He
understands English better than he speaks it, and we
had even less knowledge of French. However, he
was able to tell us of the Friends' meeting he had
attended in London, saying, 'It was there I made the
acquaintance of Allen and Grellet.' Also he told
Daniel Wheeler, 'You have indeed done a great
deal of work, Mr. Wheeler.'"

The Empress had paid a short visit a week or two
previously, and left the impression that she was of
a very "retiring character," that she wore "a pelisse
of a pretty Friendly colour," but that "her shoes
were too thin for the state of their roads at that
season." Notwithstanding her shoes, however, she
was so wishful to see the result of their few months'
treatment of the land, that she insisted on leaving her
carriage and walking about, expressing much surprise
and approbation. She did not stay to tea on that
occasion; they discovered afterwards that she was
embarrassed by the presence of the interpreter.

"Both she and the Emperor are greatly beloved
by their people." They both promised to come again,
which they did, together, when they were both at
liberty, their beautifully simple manners showing
the perfection of their politeness, which in their case,
we believe, originated in the true Christian spirit of
which mere politeness is too often only the counter-
feit.

The Emperor, as well as our English Friends, was beginning to look forward to the visit of William Allen and Stephen Grellet to Petersburg in the approaching winter. Daniel and Jane Wheeler would gladly have had them make their home at Okta during their stay if the distance from the city had not been so great, but at the meetings, which were steadily kept up on " First and Fifth days," their helpful company might certainly be hoped for.

It was in the early autumn of this first year of their experiment that Daniel Wheeler wrote to one of his Sheffield correspondents, " We are now making preparations for the winter, and have laid in a large store of wood for fuel ; much more than I should have thought it possible that we could consume. But as many fears are entertained by our friends here, lest we should suffer from the cold, we are forced to comply with their advice. The Russians keep themselves much warmer than we shall like, and I think it will be better to wear a little extra clothing than to keep our rooms so excessively heated."

" We have lately had some frosty nights, which have obliged us to try the stove in one room ; we are much pleased with its construction, and think it preferable to our open English fireplaces."

Again he writes : " I have lately been inquiring the manner in which the winter here begins, and am informed that after some cold rainy weather, the English winter commences, which freezes over parts of Lake Ladoga. These are soon broken up by the wind, when the ice comes down in large flakes and blocks up the Gulf of Finland and the Neva. Shortly after this the winter comes in reality and fixes the ice, often in a very rough state just as it has been hurried down by the current—many of the flakes lying one upon another. Often the whole becomes solid in forty-eight hours, after which roads are levelled over the rough ice at those places where the pontoon bridges and the ferries have been, which are then marked out by fir trees set up in the ice."

It is at the time of this first breaking up of the ice in Lake Ladoga—or rather of its arrival in the Neva—that the value of the pontoon bridges is best recognised. These early attracted the notice and appreciation of our English Friends, as remarks in their letters testify. They were described as composed of boats of 40 or 50 tons burden moored by two cables each, in a line across the river; over these, strong planks are laid and firmly fastened, with railing on each side, making a complete bridge. In summer, quite early in the mornings, before the traffic of wheels and foot-passengers begins, a boat is taken out of the middle and the rest are drawn aside for a certain time or until all the ships waiting to pass through have done so. And this is accomplished without any anxiety as to the width of an arch or the necessity for lowering a single mast.

In winter the whole bridge can be quickly and easily removed so that the ice may have a free passage. If it were to come to a trial of strength between a stone bridge and those large ice blocks it is scarcely necessary to say that the bridge would fare the worse of the two.

It was just about three hours after the bridge of boats had been removed for the winter in the year we are speaking of, that our Friends Allen and Grellet arrived on the further bank of the Neva, and found themselves in a great difficulty, the bridge being gone and no one seeming willing to attempt the crossing in a boat. But they felt that a supreme effort must be made to get across, for they could obtain neither bed nor food on that side, and they were cold and hungry and nearly worn out by fatigue. They knew no one yet in the city. Though they had many and valuable letters of introduction with them, there had been no opportunity for delivering any of these, and no one knew of their arrival. They had no idea, even, in which direction to turn for Okta, or their troubles would have quickly ended; so there was nothing to be done but persevere in their attempts to cross the river by some means.

After many failures a few men were at length induced to take them across in a small boat—a perilous journey, but they had no alternative—and they were favoured to retain the peaceful assurance that as they were in their present situation in obedience, as they believed, to the command of their Divine Master, they would be protected until their work was accomplished. Nevertheless it was with a feeling of deep thankfulness and content that they landed on the city side and engaging two droschkies told the drivers to take them to the Hôtel de l'Europe, where they arrived after dark.

The next day they presented certain of their letters of introduction and were well cared for in the future. The Emperor was absent from Petersburg until nearly the end of their visit, but they found that he had written to his Prime Minister, Prince Alexander Galitzin, desiring that if they came during his absence they should be treated *as his guests* and detained until his return.

The well-known consideration in which our Friends were held by the Royal family would, of course, have been sufficient to open the doors of the Russian nobles to them, but there were amongst that class a number of thoughtful, seriously-disposed individuals who cordially received them for their own sakes and heard them gladly. There was no middle class, we are told, at that time in Russia, unless, perhaps, those English merchants who lived like princes in their handsome houses were already forming a nucleus round which, after the serfs received their freedom, a useful middle class might gather. The poor our Friends would seek out for themselves.

Since leaving England they had spent four months in Norway, Sweden and Finland, and there, as elsewhere, the inspection of prisons, hospitals and schools, occupied much of their time. Their mission was rather a peculiar one; as William Allen explained to the Prime Minister, their "motives for visiting this and other countries, were no other than a sense of religious duty laid upon them by the Great Parent of the human family, and a strong desire to promote the general welfare of mankind." And with this in view he solicited permission to see the Russian public institutions, as prisons, schools, etc., which was not only readily granted, but every facility given for carrying it out.

The day after their arrival, by the kind help of some of their friends, comfortable apartments were found for our travellers in the house of an Englishwoman who had married a Russian officer, but was then a widow. Here they had many, and often very interesting visitors. " General D'junkovsky a principal officer of the Minister of the Interior called to-day," William Allen writes in his diary. " He is at the head of the department for all public buildings, and has the superintendence of Daniel Wheeler. In addition to that, as a point of mutual interest he was able to give us a good deal of information respecting the Dukhobortsi whom he had the charge of sending to the Crimea. He says that the Emperor of Russia not only protected them, but has been like a father to them. He gave us good reason for supposing that they originally came from the followers of John Huss." Judging from the account of the conversation given in the " Life of William Allen," the cause of offence seems to have been their public use of unguarded language on the subject of pictures—calling them idols—which " of itself was enough to enrage the common people," the General remarked. So far as we are acquainted with the habit of the peasant mind, we think he was right, and that Alexander's manner of treating them showed both his patience and his enlightenment.

A couple of months went by in this way, the two Friends varying their engagements in the city by visits to Okta, more or less regular according to the weather, but always bringing refreshment of spirit to the little company meeting together there.

V.

THE WOES OF A MILD WINTER.

WINTER was unusually late in its appearance in 1818, which suited our English agriculturists exactly. They were glad of the extended time for pursuing certain operations on the land, of which they would feel the value next season.

There is a memorandum extant to the effect that on the eleventh of November a strong westerly wind broke up the ice in Lake Ladoga, which came floating down for fifteen days afterwards. The date was interesting to the diary-keeper for more personal reasons as well, but these he did not mention.

As Daniel Wheeler had been told in answer to his inquiries, we may remember, *that* marked the end of what they called the English winter, and the beginning of the genuine Russian one, *which would last for six months*. Arrangements to meet it were accordingly made in good earnest. An abundant store of wood we know had been laid in. Amongst other preparations the second windows were put up, and a thermometer was hung outside, in such a position that it could be seen from the room, and consulted before leaving the house, as a guide to the amount of clothing to put on. The cold would become so intense that it would not be safe to risk stepping out to try.

They had, of course, already provided themselves with the extra garments considered necessary for out-door wear, and the descriptions of them we find in letters of this period, suggest portly figures clad with more regard to comfort than elegance. Some of the party contented themselves with Schoubs lined with sheepskins, and were agreeably surprised by the softness and silky appearance of the wool when dressed in the Russian way.

This was the resting half of the year so far as regards labour on the land : the climate decided that for all whom it concerned. The men sent by the government to work at Okta at once returned to winter quarters on the arrival of frost, for no spade can penetrate the soil when the Ice-King has taken possession of it. Our friends were therefore relieved from all responsibility on the men's account, and could usefully and pleasantly fill up their time with lessons, reading, letter-writing or private study as seemed to them best. Amusement came in their way occasionally.

In one of George's letters we read, " We watched an amusing scene to-day from our windows—a large handsome sledge full of richly-dressed ladies and gentlemen was upset just opposite the house. People are often toppled over. As we knew there was no danger and no chance of their being hurt, we could join in their hearty laughter as they rolled over and over in the snow. Their beautiful fur-lined silks were so slippery it was impossible to rise ; they could neither help each other, nor find a resting place for arm or foot by which to raise themselves. Of course we did not only laugh. As soon as we could get into

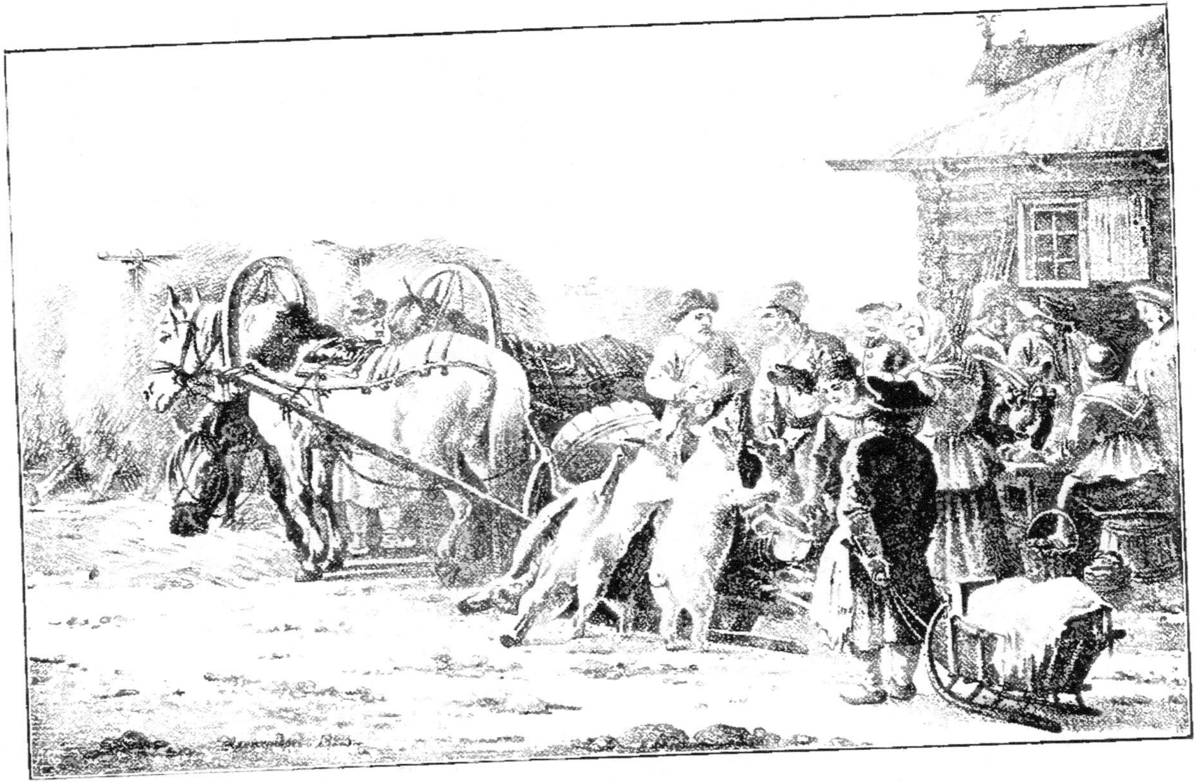

FROZEN MEAT MARKET.

our own furs we went to their aid, and quickly set them off again no worse for the adventure."

It soon became evident that the present winter was going to be a mild one—for Russia. This might be acceptable to the new-comers but for the country generally it was considered a calamity, they were told, and that experience would prove it to them.

The trouble that was quoted as likely to overtake them first, and to be felt most severely by rich and poor was that the "Frozen Market" could not be held at the usual time. Ignorance of what was meant by the "Frozen Market" prevented the due expression of sympathy for its absence that was evidently expected of them, but details were soon added, and they found it to be a most peculiar function. Great preparations were made for it every year in the somewhat vague district known as "the Interior," and the scene in Petersburg when the time arrived for holding the market—three days before Christmas—must have been curious in the extreme and not altogether pleasing.

Large stocks of cattle, sheep, pigs and poultry were killed in readiness, but instead of being salted to preserve them for future use, they were *frozen whole.*

Probably the same noblemen's estates from which the hay and other produce came drifting down the Neva in the summer, furnished the frozen provisions for the less genial season.

"When the snow sets in," our friends were told, a quantity of these curious wooden-looking animals —more than sufficient to supply all the consumption of the city for two months—would be sent by sledge to Petersburg. And the custom was for a house-

holder to purchase two or three or more whole
carcasses, according to the number of his family, and
keep them in his ice-cellar until wanted.   Then he
would in an evening chop off with an axe the joint
required for the next day's dinner, and lay it on the
stove all night to thaw.   The axe would be needed
for the flesh as well as the bone, they being equally
hard and splintery.

But this winter the snow never did "set in."
There might be sufficient in the drifts to upset a
sledge full of people into but not enough to cover the
roads to a depth sufficient for long sledging journeys.
Therefore, as the river was solid though not firm,
there remained no means of transporting the much
needed provisions to the capital.   Neither was the
frost severe enough to keep them good until they
could be eaten nearer home.   A double calamity.

It is quite possible that there are railways now
along those thousand or two versts of road, but this
simple chronicle is only concerned with what was
in existence eighty years ago. Usually at this season
sledge after sledge was to be seen conveying great
cubes of three-feet-thick ice to replenish the ice-
houses of the neighbourhood, but this year the frost
had not been strong enough to weld into good solid
masses the ice sent down the river.   The blocks,
in addition to being smaller, were less firm than was
desirable for lasting the summer through.

The ice-houses were double buildings, the internal
one, its floor covered with these blocks, having a
passage round it after the fashion of the British
Museum reading-room.   The servant was required
to shut the outer door before opening that of the

inner apartment which was visited many times a day in summer. For it was not merely a store-house of ice as a luxury for the table, but also the common larder for provisions. Boards were laid across the immense blocks of ice to hold the dishes of food, but even then it was often impossible to keep it from one day to another in the hot season.

This winter, therefore, (the mildest known for fifty years) was the harbinger of further troubles later on. The visions of slipping boards, of broken crockery and of provisions which had been left ready for the table, found swimming in cream and butter on the floor, which appeared before the eyes of those who had experience and understanding, were only too likely to be realised.

And unfortunately this does not exhaust the list of troubles for which a mild winter is answerable in Russia. The same deficient carpeting of snow which affected commerce so injuriously also placed a difficulty in the way of sledging for pleasure, and sledging, when all goes well is a *great* pleasure—a delightful means of locomotion. But the "when" is a necessary provision. The gliding along during the first few weeks of a normal winter while the snow is smooth and hard, or during the whole winter on the unfrequented roads, is like that of a boat in calm water, but when the ice and snow have been cut up by much travelling it is more like the same boat on a billowy sea, to most people decidedly less pleasant.

One winter while our friends were in Russia the deeply-snow-covered road between Petersburg and Moscow was worn so full of holes by the sledges that many people were thoroughly sea-sick on the journey.

Sledges were very handsome-looking conveyances; their strong frame-work was only rough, it is true, but when a richly-coloured carpet was thrown over the back, and plenty of furs about the feet and knees the general appearance was truly luxurious. The best of them were, like the carriages in summer, drawn by three horses abreast; or to speak correctly, they were *drawn* by one horse trotting in the shafts, accompanied by two others outside them, whose business it was to gallop gracefully one on the right the other on the left, at the same time bending their heads away from the shaft-horse with a peculiar turn which had a very showy effect. This was, of course, the result of long patient training, and each side horse could only run on the side for which it had been trained. The head of the middle one was held high by a bearing rein carried over a lofty arched collar; all three horses having long glossy tails, and being affectionately cared for, their appearance was splendid. It is a plan that, fortunately for the horses, could only be adopted in a country where horses are plentiful and space ample, but it seems to be still kept up in the Imperial City of the North.

An affecting incident is narrated in one of the letters written about this time connected with "Blessing the Waters of the Neva." It is an important ceremony and crowds of people assemble to watch the procession of priests of the Greek church. A hole has previously been cut in the ice which covers the beautiful blue water to the thickness of two or three feet according to the severity of the season. On reaching the river, a priest, after reading a short portion of Scripture, thrice dips into the stream a hollow cross. The water that drops from this is deemed specially precious, and happy are the favoured few who are near enough to catch some of it ; they consider themselves safe from illness and many other troubles for the next twelve months. The priest then dips a bundle of birch twigs into the water and sprinkles all within reach ; after this babies are brought to him by their devoted mothers who think they will be blest for life, poor little things, by a plunge into the cold stream.

The priest, this year, was unfortunate or unskilful enough to lose hold of one little foot, and the strong current quickly carried the babe far away beneath the ice. He lost no time in regrets or apologies, or even consolation ; but turned to the bereaved woman, and calmly saying, " The Lord has taken it," held out his hand for the next.

Stranger still was the fact that the mother accepted his version, and considered herself an object for envy rather than commiseration.

All too soon for their own pleasure the time arrived when our Friends at Okta were called upon to bid farewell to the two companions, Allen and Grellet, who had so often brightened for them the dark days of this, their first winter in Russia.

" They left us ten days ago," Daniel Wheeler writes to a Friend at Hull. " I saw them off from the city just at the edge of dark, in a covered sledge in the midst of a heavy snow-storm." " As they travel night and day, it seems to give them a nice stretch of daylight for their final preparations," George explains in a letter home in reference to the peculiar time of their departure. " They found a purchaser in Petersburg

for the carriage they took with them from England,"
he goes on to say, "and bought a large covered sledge,
called a Cabitka or Kibitka, which was better suited for
their long continued journeys. Their luggage was
put in the bottom of the sledge, and over it a bed
covered with black morocco leather, on which they
could either sit or lie down."

" They had also provisions with them, and a servant
able to speak French, German and Russian. They
were furnished with letters and papers sufficient to
open the way wherever they go, and finally a docu-
ment which obliges the postmasters to furnish them
with horses as soon as they arrive." In fact everything that could be thought of was provided by the
Emperor's direction for the futherance of their objects.
Their intention was to go first to Moscow, then to the
Crimea, Constantinople, Italy, etc., their motives for
undertaking the journey being, as has already been
stated, " a sense of religious duty and a strong desire
to promote the general welfare of mankind."

Letters were received from the travellers, but we
cannot follow their progress further on the present
occasion, as our special interest is centered on the
transformation work going on at Okta during this
remarkable winter.

VI.

VOLKOVO.

THE " transformation " at Okta had been steadily progressing. George writes, " The part which last year presented only the appearance of a boggy, moorish tract of land is now an enclosed field covered with rich vegetables." Even Daniel Wheeler was much impressed by the rapidity with which vegetation came to maturity when once the frost was out of the ground. " Grass, twelve weeks after sowing, was in full flower, looking like a good crop the *year* after sowing in England."

It must not be forgotten that they had only to ask for what they considered necessary, whether in implements or stock, and it was supplied to them without hesitation and without question. Neither must we forget that a more important factor still in the pleasing and astonishing result exhibited in this, their second summer, was the earnest, unflagging attention given by them to the work.

The Emperor had long desired to accomplish this plan of draining and cultivating the land around the city, and even before he visited England he had attempted to carry it out, but, unfortunately, the persons he employed seem to have been both ignorant and unscrupulous. His second experiment proved more successful. Under the present management, not only was there a more satisfactory result to show, but also it was achieved at less cost, notwithstanding the liberality with which our friends were treated. The Okta produce certainly bore the palm in the Petersburg market—their hay and vegetables fetched higher prices than any other, and Daniel Wheeler says, " We cannot supply the demand quickly enough."

That the owners of neighbouring estates noticed and appreciated the good result of the English farmers' plans was evident from his further remark, "The little progress we have made is at once copied by the landed proprietors around the village of Okta." This was so far gratifying, but he thought still more might be done in the direction of example.

It had been intended that as the land came into cultivation, Daniel Wheeler should continue to farm it, but a better plan and one more pleasing to him was, in the end, adopted. We will try to describe it.

We have more than once alluded to the condition of the serfs at that time, which was, in fact, a species of slavery. The claims both on their time and their earnings were arbitrary and variable, and as a consequence the people had no interest in anything. Daniel Wheeler writes, " I have heard it said among them that 'life is not worth a kopek'"—the hundredth part of a shilling—which was to him " a very affecting circumstance." His compassion led to the idea of giving them an interest in the land.

He proposed to divide the Okta plot into small farms from thirty to forty-five acres each, with the exception of one which should be at least double the size of the rest, and to erect a farm-house and outbuildings on each according to the amount of land. The large farm with its more complete establishment was to be kept in the hands of the government, and worked as an example of the best way of proceeding. The others, he hoped, might be let to suitable peasants at a moderate rent, but at the same time one sufficient to pay ordinary interest on the money laid out in draining, cultivating and building. When the rent had been paid the remainder of the profits would be the tenant's own, but owing to their inexperience in agricultural pursuits there might probably, in the first instance, be certain restrictions needful as to the management of the land.

Daniel Wheeler had spent part of the winter's leisure in making a model for one of these farm-houses which he hoped to see erected the following summer, and when they were happily occupied he trusted the peasants would find there *was* something worth living for after all. He also " hoped that the nobles would see it to their interest to divide their large estates in a similar manner, and place their peasants on the same footing," adding, " I am persuaded their income would be greatly increased." It would be exceedingly interesting to know the state of the Okta village now.

Daniel Wheeler had been very wishful to call the little colony " The Free Village," but though he was allowed full liberty as to its construction, that name could *not* be permitted.

Arrangements being so far advanced for the completion of the first instalment of their work, it was time to take a look at the land which was next to be brought under cultivation. It was a large district called Volkovo, situated on the south side of the city.

Daniel Wheeler and his lieutenant (as he used to call George), therefore made an excursion one day in that second summer to inspect it and take a few rough measurements and levels as guides for arranging the order of proceeding. It was now quite settled that William Wheeler and the young tutor were to exchange places : the latter was better able to bear the varied weather, and the former, in addition to instructing his brothers and sisters, found abundant opportunities for helping his father by his thoughtful care at home. George had superintended much of the draining work at Okta, and as draining must be the first and indeed the only operation which could be carried on this year at Volkovo, Daniel Wheeler decided to give him the charge of a couple of hundred men, and throw him on his own responsibility to prepare the ground for general cultivation the year following. There was only one difficulty, to be considered later.

They found a great part of the land excellent and only needing enclosing ; for which purpose there were thousands of straight young fir trees waiting to be cut down for posts and fencing. There was a large extent of bog compared with Okta, but not when compared with the whole area at Volkovo, and there were very extensive woods. George thought "the plot would be about 50,000 acres," but whether fifty times the size of the Okta land was a probable guess or not we cannot tell, not having met with a definite measurement of the new piece. He speaks incidentally of ten miles of drain wanted, and two miles of road, also of sixty-four acres of hundred-year-old roots to be grubbed up, which

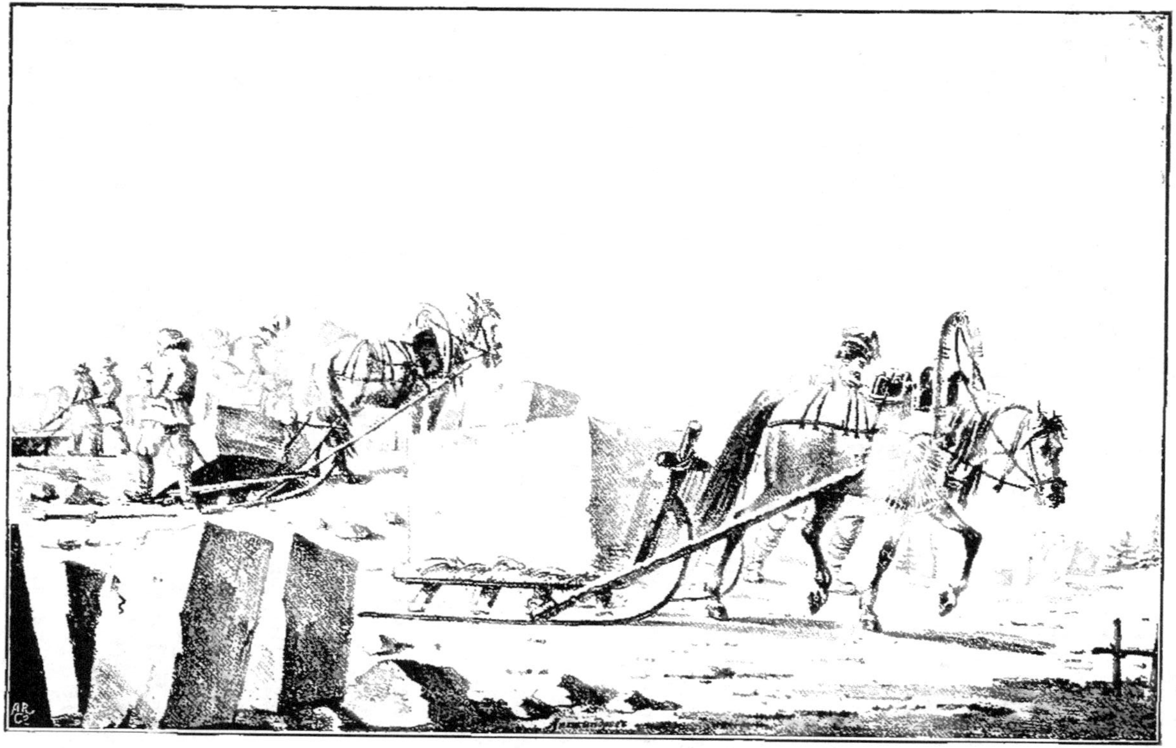

ICE-BLOCKS FROM THE NEVA.

amounts give the idea of an extensive tract at any rate.

There was nothing either in the kind of work to be done, or the amount of it, to embarrass the young man after his last year's experience at Okta,—the difficulty that presented itself to their minds was, where he could lay his head when the day's work was over.

In the first place, there was no house on the land. It had previously been decided that the following year (1820) it would be desirable for Daniel Wheeler and his family, with two exceptions, to remove nearer to the new work. The nearest house that could be found at all suitable for them was one on the Moscow road, belonging to Count Romanzoff. This, they were informed would be at their service whenever they were ready for it, but it was quite too large for a lone young man to occupy even for the four months he and his men expected to be at work there, and one of the objects of their present excursion was to see what could be done to make him comfortable.

The literal " bed and board " required for the men could easily be supplied, but the only shelter visible for their director was a small wooden house inhabited by an old Russian peasant who lived quite alone and did everything for himself. He was a venerable-looking old man whose white beard and simple dress gave him a patriarchal, almost a hermit-like appearance. Here George could be accommodated with a lodging, and be saved a great deal of fatigue if he would manage to cook for himself.

Considering the circumstances—that they were

eight miles from Okta, too far to go and come each day, as they began work at five in the morning, and that the village of Volkovo was equally distant in another direction and of course equally inconvenient, —he was not only willing, but he preferred to try and cook for himself rather than run the risk of what he might otherwise be called upon to eat. He had been an Ackworth scholar in Ackworth's Spartan days, and though cookery was not one of the subjects taught at that establishment, the domestic knowledge of various kinds that the boys could not help picking up there, added to a little common sense, enabled him to get along quite easily, when the experiment was tried later on.

After finishing their levelling and arranging domestic affairs as well as circumstances would allow, they turned their steps to the city. Their daily occupations left but scant leisure for making themselves acquainted with its grandeur, both of space and architecture, so that the walk through its miles of handsome streets felt like a well-earned holiday. General D'junkovsky lived in the city, and they were invited to dine with him. He and Daniel Wheeler had a great deal to do with each other, and their mutual feelings were those of admiration and esteem.

Dinner was, of course, served *à la Russe*, and the account given to a correspondent by the younger guest is very amusing though not worth repeating in these days. That the list of dishes ended with an English apple pie served *à l'Anglaise* was intended as a compliment no doubt ; but the concluding ceremony after the meal was essentially Russian, or—on second thoughts—was it perhaps old English too ?

Each guest after crossing himself, bowed to the master and mistress of the house, thanking them for their entertainment, they in return bowing and thanking the guests for their company. It was an incident for George to remember when he was eating his solitary dinners the next week at Volkovo —for no time must be lost now that the final arrangements were decided on. There could scarcely have been contrived a more complete contrast. For the next four months this was George's morning routine :—he rose at four, made his bed, swept his room with a bundle of birch twigs, prepared breakfast, and left all as tidy as if he expected a daily visit from the Emperor. "External dirt and disorder," he used to say, "tended to a disorderly state of mind." In like manner he went on through the day, contenting himself with what seemed the best arrangement possible for the time, and all the more intensely enjoying the weekly refreshment of English conversation at Okta.

In the interval between those Okta talks, there were two visits from Daniel Wheeler to look forward to each week, when, as he said, he brought " provisions to the garrison," and generally on these occasions shared such a dinner as the " cook " was able to provide. He managed to get a good deal of amusement out of George's " handy ways," as he used to call them, often quoting to him the well-known couplet

"At once the sage, the hero and the cook,
He wields the (spade) the saucepan and the book."

" Doctor" might very appropriately have been added to the list of characters that the lieutenant played in turn, for being really interested in his men,

he was often appealed to for help in sickness, and he
still found " common sense " the most valuable ally
in deciding questions, either medical or culinary. For
instance, Petrof, one of the men, had taken the opportunity of a fête-day to fetch from a little distance a
basket of oranges. These fête-days were numerous,
and were all well kept as holidays—another hindrance
to steady work. Whether Petrof was commercially
inclined or what was his object does not appear, but
he told George on his return he was very sorry he had
bought the oranges, for there was an evil spirit
amongst them. It had been singing in the basket all
the way home, and it would not leave him, sometimes
it was singing and sometimes dancing before him like
a little black imp.

George strongly suspected there had been an evil
spirit somewhere, if not amongst the oranges ; however,
he saw the man had a severe cold, and prescribed for
him accordingly. He was to go home,—he lived in
the village—get his wife to make some tea, and was
to drink not *less* than fifteen cups of it ; then he was
to wrap himself in his schoub, and lie down on the
top of the stove ! One other order the amateur doctor
thought it wise to add, knowing by this time the
habits of the people : Petrof was *not* on any account
to get up in the night, and roll himself in the snow ;
if he did, he would be sure to meet the evil spirit, and
the consequences might be serious ! He was obedient,
happily, and came back to work very thankful to his
young commander, and wonderfully impressed by his
powers of exorcising the wicked one.

Another time one of his men addressed him as they
met on the land, " Yagor Ivanovitch, is it permitted

to go to my master, and ask to have a tooth taken out ? " The poor man's cheek was swollen to double its usual size, his eyes were bloodshot, and his whole appearance denoted great suffering.

" Put on thy cap, my friend, in the first place," said George, " and then tell me whose tooth thou art talking about. It is eighty miles to thy master's estate, and I do not know what thou means. Is it thy master's tooth or thy own ? "

" It is my master's tooth, Yagor Ivanovitch, but it is in this head," putting his hand up to his cheek. " I am entirely my master's property, and can do nothing without his leave."

According to the letter of the law, George found this to be correct, but he ventured to take the responsibility of giving permission for the extraction of the offending tooth, if poor Alexis could find someone amongst his comrades who could relieve him of it. Dentistry, George feared, was beyond his own powers.

VII.

GOOD NEWS.

GEORGE found the loneliness of life at Volkovo more trying than he anticipated. For the greater part of each week no word of English passed his lips, and the few remarks exchanged in Russ between himself and the old patriarch were not of a lively character, while the other human beings with whom he held intercourse —his two hundred men—were possessed of ideas even less enlivening than those of his white-haired landlord. The work was no longer a novelty, it had become mere routine, there was nothing to do but to think, to picture old scenes, and to listen, in fancy, to the voice which had exerted so powerful an influence over him.

He had determined to keep up, if possible, a correspondence with his old master at Broomhall, although he was forbidden to write to the daughter, and his first letter from the new country had been kindly and promptly replied to, but his second communication had met with no response. An almost crushing disappointment in connection with this had awaited him on his last "week-end" visit to Okta. Even *his* buoyant spirit had not been able to withstand its effects. He felt thoroughly depressed.

A parcel of English letters just received by a "private opportunity" was being distributed as he entered the Okta sitting-room on the previous "First-day" afternoon. Three of them were smilingly handed to himself, one from his sister, one from the fellow-townsman he had left at Sheffield in William Fairbank's office, and the word Petersburg just visible on the third as he held them in his hand was certainly in William Singleton's writing. This he opened first without further examination, but instantly discovered that it was intended for Daniel Wheeler, to whom, of course, he at once took it, with many apologies for his carelessness. It was very tantalising but George still hoped for a message for himself. Unfortunately tea was announced at that moment, the evening meeting followed, and immediately afterwards it was time for him to set out on his eight miles' walk back to Volkovo.

"Farewell, George," Daniel Wheeler said at parting, "I intend to come and see thee on Third-day, and bring the usual provisions, and something——" He checked himself in what he was going to say, repeating "provisions," etc.

"Am I to expect something more than usual?" George ventured to ask, hoping for a message of remembrance, if nothing else.

"Thou wilt see," replied his friend with a significant smile. That was the only clue he gave to the nature of the "something," and George was obliged to go.

Therefore, when dinner-time came and passed on "Third-day" without any sign of Daniel Wheeler, poor George felt sure that all was over. And when

the expected visitor appeared later in the afternoon
—having been detained in the city on his way—and
still did not seem to have any message to deliver,
George's returning hope, brighter for the moment on
seeing his friend, again faded. His honest face
could not help expressing something of his gloomy
feelings, and must at last have touched his companion's sympathy,—or perhaps his compassion ; if it
had been real sympathy he surely would not have kept
the young man so long in suspense. The ways of our
grandparents are often inscrutable to the present
generation, as our habits of thought and action may
in turn be equally a puzzle to our own descendants.

" What art thou going to do this afternoon,
George ? " Daniel Wheeler asked, as he prepared to
depart, " in this pouring rain it is of no use to return
to the land, the men will have left work. Suppose
thou wert to sit down and pen a long letter to Anne
Singleton ? " George looked so searchingly into his
face that he felt it was time to be serious.

" Yes, my dear young friend, her father desires
me to tell thee that they withdraw their prohibition ;
her mother sends thee her good wishes, and I need
not add that both of you have mine."

Daniel Wheeler only lingered long enough after
imparting his good news to satisfy his young friend's
curiosity as to how the change was brought about. It
seemed that the number of persons interested in the
young people was larger than the lady's parents
imagined, and the kind expressions in George's favour
which came dropping in, had at length produced the
desired effect. He felt very grateful and, of course,
very happy.

Two years elapsed before he was ready to fetch his bride, but he occupied himself with preparing a home for her, and never lost his spirits again.

The winter of 1819-20, which came suddenly upon them soon after this and stopped all their out-door work, proved as remarkable for its severity as their first winter had been for its mildness. They felt the difference in various directions. It demanded still more clothing out of doors. A sort of cloak lined with hyæna skins was put on over all the other garments, more voluminous fur-lined boots worn over the ordinary ones, and fur caps and gloves more thickly padded with cotton-wool, we read of in that season's letters.

The wearer's personal appearance was of very secondary importance in their own eyes we know, and truly it was well for them they did not care about it, for they must have looked curious objects when prepared to brave the outer air. But with all this extra covering there remained one prominent feature that it was scarcely possible to protect, and our friends quickly learned the lesson that a man's nose could be seriously frost bitten, and he be perfectly unconscious of what was going on. Therefore it became usual in a severe winter to notice the colour of the nose and ears (if these were visible) on the faces of people they met. If on either one or the other the peculiar whiteness that denotes danger were recognized, " Your nose or your ear is frozen, sir," would be the kindest of all salutations in passing. Even the rougher style of intimating the fact which was sometimes adopted—that of seizing a handful of snow and rubbing the affected member therewith—would give

no offence, for none would be meant. It would only
be thought the correct treatment applied with somewhat needless energy.

Of course, George had returned to Okta when the
frost drove the workers from the ground at Volkovo,
not at all sorry to give up his hermit-like existence. He
resumed the plan of devoting four hours a day to
instructing the younger members of the family, and
pursued his own studies and letter-writing in his
leisure time. The long winter recess, if we may call
it so, was a most valuable help to him. He wrote to
his sister at this time, " you say you are having a hard
winter, and wonder what is our experience as regards
weather. We, too, are making acquaintance with an
unusually severe season even for Russia ; but we can
clothe ourselves so much more sensibly for the end in
view than you have opportunity for doing, that, I
fancy, notwithstanding the different reports that your
thermometer and ours must be giving of the state of
the atmosphere outside, you have felt the cold more
than we have." And he proceeds to describe much the
same outfit as the one already spoken of above. But, he
goes on to say, he is only referring to people and, in connection with them, the domestic animals under their
care. The wild creatures often suffer intensely. " The
poor little birds, in attempting to fly, suddenly find
their wings frozen, and fall heavily to the ground,
dead. We have witnessed this happen again and
again from our windows. . . . The wolves are
growing very bold ; we have seen one pass down the
frozen river just below us, and another was shot close
to Okta. A number of men known as wolf-shooters
are always kept in the pay of the Russian government,

and if the animals become too obtrusive, an application for help is all that will be needed. Men would be sent down, and the neighbourhood soon cleared." He thought they might be obliged to make the application, as six wolves had sallied forth one night, and killed a number of horses in a field not far away. How the horses happened to be left out in the field all night he did not seem to know ; they were not horses from the Okta farm.

This record winter was followed by an unusually hot summer, making everything as dry as tinder. The transition from one season to the other, winter to summer, as well as summer to winter, was generally abrupt, but this year it was startling, even for the neighbourhood of Petersburg—and late. At the beginning of the second week in June, the trees were bare and brown, spreading their leafless branches against a dull grey sky ; by the end of the same week the brown buds had burst into leaf, and the trees stood in the bright sunshine, full-foliaged and delicately green. But the foreigners preferred the leisurely unfolding of beauty as seen in our lovely English springtime.

It was a busy summer. The plan for Daniel Wheeler's change of residence was carried out. His two older sons, William and Joshua, were conveniently provided for at the Okta house on the bank of the Neva, and the rest of the family removed to the one belonging to Count Romanzoff, while in the interval before they were ready to take possession, George occupied it alone after all.

"Thou mayst be sure," he writes to one of his brothers, "that I look forward to their arrival with the greatest pleasure, as it will prove, once more, the termination of my ascetic life."

The address heading the letters received during the next three or four years was " Fifth verst, Moscow Road," as if the house had no name of its own, and there was no neighbouring village to lend it one. It was mentioned in the last chapter as the only dwelling within reasonable distance of the changed locality of their work, and for that reason was accepted by the family in their usual uncomplaining manner. But though a large, good building in many respects, it was a cold house, and not conducive either to their comfort or good health. Its roof was of sheet iron, which, during the winter of 1820-21, was more than once considerably damaged by the prevalent strong west winds which were the distinguishing feature of that, the third Russian winter our friends passed through. At least thirty square yards were, on one occasion, blown away from the roof, and could not be replaced until warmer weather, as iron in that condition treated the workmen's fingers as if it had been red-hot. Therefore we are not surprised to find the remark in a letter from Daniel Wheeler to a friend in Doncaster, that " sickness has hung about our dwelling since the middle of last winter," nor to hear later that it had seemed necessary for his wife and daughters and son Joshua to try what a temporary return to the English climate would do for them.

During the period of this great loneliness, in their absence, Daniel Wheeler had a long, pleasant call from the Emperor. He looked serious when he heard of the indisposition of the family generally, and of the absence of so many of them in England, expressing a hope that they intended to return. "The next day he seems to have made inquiry as to the cause of the family's failing health, and having learned that it was occasioned by the coldness of the house in which we live, he gave orders that it should be altered immediately. On the third day after the interview, an architect arrived to ascertain what was wanted, and we are now well stocked with bricklayers, carpenters, etc."

The query will persistently intrude on one's mind whether it would not have been better, knowing the Emperor's feelings towards them all, respectfully to tell him of the state of things before it became so dangerous? Of one thing, however, we may be certain, the line of conduct Daniel Wheeler adopted he thought to be the line of duty, and we have no right to judge him.

Before the end of that year (1821), George had very gratifying personal experience of the Emperor's kindness and consideration. The Okta farms were being occupied as quickly as they could be prepared for tenants, and the larger dwelling-house on the double quantity of land was progressing specially with a view to its being the home of the tutor and his bride—it was hoped, the following year. The intention seemed to be generally known and to prove generally interesting, but George scarcely expected that the kind interest would extend to the Emperor. He was, however, called one day to speak to him.

"Yagor Ivanovitch," the Emperor at once addressed him, "I hear you are intending to return to England for a wife."

"That is true," replied George, "with the permission of the Emperor."

"And could you not, in my wide dominions, find a lady to suit you, that you are going to take this long journey merely to fetch one ? "

It was a question the young man scarcely knew how to answer, but Alexander came to his relief by adding—" Perhaps it has been a long engagement ? " to which he could truly reply that it had,—a long attachment at least.

" Keep it up then by all means ; but bring the lady here, do not be tempted to remain in England. I do not like to lose honest men out of my empire. When are you going ? "

As soon as the harvest was over, George replied ; but the Emperor objected that the storms would then have set in, and desired him not to mind the harvest that year, but go early in the safer and pleasanter weather. But, though naturally much gratified by the personal expression of his Imperial master's kind thought, he could not entertain the idea of neglecting his duties.

George fancied there was a more melancholy expression on Alexander's face than when they first met, and considering the weight of his responsibility he was not surprised.

Having helped to see the harvest in, George started for England and secured his bride before the close of 1821.

VIII.

SETTLING IN AT THE NEW HOME.

PLEASANT as was the quiet resting-time enjoyed after their marriage by the young couple in whom we are just now interested, they both felt that, as soon as the Baltic was once more open to the passage of vessels, there must be no unnecessary delay in starting on their journey. The right to care on one side, and to be cared for on the other, was still a delightful novelty, but they looked forward hopefully to a lifetime of that enjoyment, and, in any case, there would be the two or three weeks of the voyage in which to do nothing else.

The bride was to be accompanied by one of her younger sisters that she might, at first at least, have an English-speaking companion at hand in the hours of her husband's absence. They were all invited to spend a fortnight at the house on the Moscow Road, as their own was not quite ready for their reception, and the various members of the Wheeler family were in a state of pleasant anticipation. The younger daughter of the house had assumed the post of honorary sentinel, and patiently watched for the first sign of their approach. At last, after two days of disappointment, the cry was heard of " Here they come ! here they come ! They are driving down the Moscow Road, in a carriage and four and two horses ! "

" What are the four then if they have only two horses, Janingka ? " asked an older brother.

" Four wheels of course ; I thought that was it because many of the droschkies have only two," promptly replied Janingka, *Anglicé* little Jane.

" She has perhaps never seen four horses in use," suggested another brother, " she does not remember much of England, and here the good carriages have three abreast, you know, the showy side ones turning their heads away from the real worker in the middle."

" Perhaps so, and there is more sense in her description than we gave her credit for," added the first speaker.

By this time the carriage and " four " had reached the house, and the long expected travellers, George and Anne Edmondson, and Anne's younger sister Sarah, were received by the assembled family as if they had been near and dear relations. One of the greatest deprivations of their situation was the rarity of opportunities for intelligence from " home."

It had been decided that the two younger boys, Charles and Daniel, were to live with their tutor in the new house at Okta, and they remembered sufficient of the life at Broomhall to be quite satisfied with the arrangement. Their elder sister felt that now *she* might hope for a companion, and the heads of the family were secretly longing for the opening of the budget of news from England.

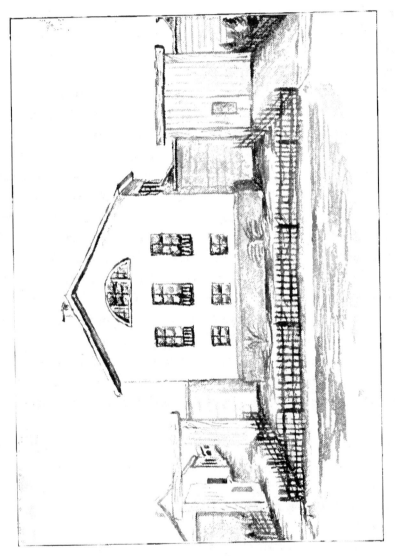

ESTABLISHMENT HOUSE.

Every one was ready to give a warm welcome to the new-comers. They passed the next fortnight very pleasantly, yet, at the end of that time, they were not sorry to move with Theodosia, their Russian servant, to the new home, hoping to settle down there in peace and happiness.

"Establishment House" was the rather peculiar name that had been given to the new dwelling. We do not know who was answerable for it. It was, perhaps, simply the translation of some more euphonious Russian word, and one name would do as well as another, they thought, if the place proved comfortable. The house was built of fir trees laid one upon another and neatly jointed at the corners. On the outside these were covered with planks which were nicely painted ; inside the interstices were stuffed with moss, and the whole faced with canvas and coloured. Such building was customary, and, when complete, made a thoroughly warm respectable looking house. This one consisted of the usual two stories. There were four rather low but good-sized apartments on the ground floor, two of them for the men who had charge of the horses, the other two for granary and harness-room. The upper story was to be occupied by the family, according to custom.

Unfortunately, when the family came to take possession of it, they found that a tribe of invaders had been beforehand with them,—the rooms were already swarming with occupants. There was a long struggle for supremacy with the insect army, which interfered during many weeks with the hoped for peaceful happiness. The rightful owners made a temporary surrender of the premises, the warm season allowing them to occupy a tent while the walls of their house were stripped to the wood and re-stuffed with fresh moss. Instead of canvas they were then covered with plaster, other quarters were found for the men whose rooms would have kept up a supply of the invaders, and the final result was satisfactory.

Theodosia wondered that they should take all this trouble to get rid of such harmless little creatures as those they were combating, and, in fact, was surprised that the family should object to their presence in the house at all, and many of their neighbours shared Theodosia's views, but our trio were content with their work.

" The bustle of settling in," the sisters called this little episode in writing home, and they did not say much about it, wisely preferring to send only pleasant pictures. They told of the handsome stable for fourteen horses, of the little flower-border round the yard where they had sown the seeds they brought from England. Every one of them had lived and prospered, each a memento of some friend or familiar locality. Even the rhubarb was showing its large leaves. They would send in return seeds of the Russian larkspurs which were very beautiful.

The mistress of the house described triumphantly the rustic fence round the large kitchen-garden that her husband had made " with his own hands," and the ornamental gateway to the new ice-house, which she seemed to admire very much. She had evidently made up her mind to look on the bright side of things. À *propos* of the ice-houses, he mentioned that the July before she came, George had found thick ice under one of the heaps of sphagnum, (spoken of in an earlier chapter), which had suggested to him the idea of covering the ice-blocks this summer with a deep layer of the same kind of moss.   It was proving a great success ; the surface of the ice, on which so much of their comfort depended in hot weather, was remaining cool and firm.   " Another triumph for George ! "

The routine of his daily life was a little altered in his new position, but it was still very simple, and the hours were primitive.   One item was an exceedingly annoying one ; at each farm-yard meal it was necessary to stand by and see the food actually eaten by the animals.   It was not enough to give out the oats, etc., if the master would be certain that they were honestly used, he must stand by and watch.   No bailiff or overlooker could be found with any better principles than the men had themselves, so that it was George's unpleasant duty to attend personally to this on the model farm.   There is no doubt that their personal attention was the secret of the English farmers' success.   Their hay fetched the highest price in the market, and the Okta-fed mutton, though from Russian sheep, was famous throughout the city. Good prices, with profits honestly paid to the government untaxed for bribes or other blackmail, told in a manner that was almost bewildering to the official mind.

To return to the daily routine—having, like a good farmer, superintended the breakfasts of the various animals, George sat down with a right good appetite to his own.   This, and their morning Scripture reading finished, his horse was brought to the door, and he

rode to the soldiers' quarters about a mile away.
Here the men were drawn up in line waiting for him
to count them. After giving the orders for the day
to the corporal, he rode round to the various depart-
ments to see that they were attended to—a very
necessary precaution. He dined when the men did,
at noon. In the heat of the summer they had a three
hours' recess after this meal, otherwise they only allowed themselves one hour. At four the men broke
off for further refreshment, when George went home
for a cup of tea and afterwards returned with his
workers to the fields until eight. At that hour he
paid them, saw the animals fed again, entered in a
book the amount of work done that day, took one
more look round, and then, we can easily believe, was
ready to retire to rest.

One afternoon in the following summer, George's
siesta was disturbed by a summons to the fields ; one
of the long heaps of moss had caught fire, and was
burning furiously. Our Quaker farmers first made
acquaintance with this moss, we may remember, as it
covered, to nearly a foot and a half in depth, the
boggy ground they had come over to cultivate. They
cut long drains through the land, and left them during
the winter to quietly do their work, and the following
spring carried out their plans for treating the
sphagnum. The result was astonishing. The fields
into which they divided the land were only eight
acres in extent, yet from each they had obtained two
heaps of moss, measuring, on an average, fourteen feet
in width, half that in height, and more than eight
hundred feet in length. These ridges were laid in
pairs on a convenient part of the field from which

they were gathered, and between the two was an equally long line of old tree roots, which had been dug up from a lower depth of the same ground.

The scorching sun of 1823 must have completed the drying process, and brought the heaps into a prime condition for carrying on the conflagration which rapidly spread over fifteen or sixteen acres, and seemed, at the rate at which it was travelling, to threaten the village of Okta. In addition to that danger there were the neighbouring powder-mills to consider, and if the earth itself should once take fire, no one could predict the end of the mischief. The soil was so full of roots and fibres, that it would burn like the woods above it.

In later years there were much more extensive fires than this, particularly in the hot summer of 1826, but they were chiefly on the wide Shoosharry bogs and moors, further removed from civilization. At Okta the cultivators were not permitted even to burn the rubbish from the fields, so much was a fire dreaded on account of the danger to the powder magazines, and here was the enemy suddenly amongst them, notwithstanding all their care !

The danger was sufficient, however, to give the men, for once, a rousing impetus for work. A couple of hundred soldiers were soon on the spot and got the fire so far under control that they could bear to stand near its edge, cutting away the earth down to the layer of clay, and thus surrounding the burning fields with a cold damp zone that proved an effective barrier to the enemy's advance. It was an anxious time for a few hours. Happily, however, about ten o'clock the wind abated, and George thankfully

returned home having ventured to leave sentinels
on the watch until early morning, when the men
returned to the attack and no further damage
resulted.

Since there had been a mistress of George's home,
we find more of the letters of that date in her hand-
writing than in her husband's. The time he used
to spend in letter-writing he devoted to her, while
she took up the pen he laid down, and the items
she reports are still, as at first, the happenings of
their simple but somewhat uncommon lives,—just
what the "folks at home" would desire to hear.
In one letter we have an account of the "First-day"
evening rambles, during which they sometimes
called on the families in the houses of the model
village. "In one house," she says, "there are four
generations. The representative of the oldest is a
woman 100 years old. She is blind, lame and deaf,
but finds no difficulty in the use of her tongue. The
people are very hospitable, the first question being
'what can I set before you'? One woman offered
a choice between fresh butter and eggs : another
spread a clean cloth and brought out a plate of blue-
berries, a fruit larger and more acid than our
bilberries. All seemed friendly and pleased to see
us." "Some of them have been wishing George
'many years of good health,' because of a causeway
he has made at the side of the road, which they find
a great convenience. In wet weather he used to be
troubled with foot-passengers encroaching gradually
on the fields in search of a better path. You know
exactly what would be his way of managing such
people. He first made them a better road and then

requested them to keep to it.   He says he has received
many an old woman's blessing for it."

On the arrival of the young couple from England
it had been proposed, we may remember, that Daniel
Wheeler's two younger sons should live with them,
but, in the end, the two daughters seem to have
been added to the circle as well, forming, with
Anne's sister Sarah, a lively and busy family.

IX

THE GREAT INUNDATION.

THE even tenor of these simple hard-working lives was pursued through the following year (1824) until nearly its close, both at Volkovo and the Model Farm at Okta. Then on the seventh of November (O.S.), in that year there came to the inhabitants of Petersburg "the most awful visitation that has ever occurred within the memory of the oldest person living," in the shape of a deluge which threatened for several hours the complete destruction of the city and suburbs.

The "Great Inundation" has since furnished a chapter in Russian national history, but we venture, nevertheless, to record some of the details here, thinking that incidents found in the letters written home at that time, or in the Journals of our Friends who witnessed the scenes, help one to realise more vividly than any newspaper paragraph, the state to which that splendid capital was so suddenly reduced.

A letter from Daniel Wheeler to his friend John Hipsley of Hull, dated eleventh of eleventh month, 1824, gives the most circumstantial account we have seen of the fearful state of things, as it came gradually to the knowledge of our friends at Volkovo. We have therefore made liberal use of it in the following sketch, adding only a few details from an earlier note, which George promptly sent home to assure his parents of the safety of both families.

"A terrible tempest came on during the night of the sixth, and continued to rage with unabated fury nearly the whole of the next day. Two days previously an unusual roaring of the sea had been noticed about the head of the Gulf of Finland and at Cronstadt. On the morning of the seventh, the sea began to rise and shortly afterwards to push its waves into the heart of the city. The people at first supposed it would only be one of the floods which have frequently occurred, and manifested no particular alarm, but before noon they became convinced of the necessity of flying for their lives. The road we lived on exhibited a scene of terror and dismay not easy to describe, every one anxious to save himself and his cattle.

"As our situation is somewhat higher than the city itself, we had many applications for food for the cattle and shelter, which of course we were glad to comply with. Our neighbourhood was prevented from sharing in the general calamity by the bank of the Ligofsky canal, which is raised above the regular surface of the country, but from the upper part of the house, we could see over the bank, which discovered to us the city standing, as it were, in the open sea.

That same seventh of November, Stepan was due at Okta to fetch some sheep for the market. Daniel Wheeler allowed him to undertake the journey, not at all aware of the difficulties he would encounter. It is true the Moscow road had presented all the day before an appearance of alarm and confusion, people flying with their carriages, horses, cattle, and whatsoever they could seize upon, in the sudden panic, yet the full extent of the ruin and loss of life in the city did not enter into the conception of our friends at the Farm.

In the course of an hour Stepan returned, saying there was no chance of reaching the city, the three bridges of boats across the Neva were driven from their moorings, and so much damaged they were quite unfit for use. Part of one of them was left standing against the wall of the palace : rafts, small boats, and two of the steam-boats employed in going to Cronstadt, were left in the city on " what is called the island." Here the effects of the deluge were most severely felt ; the water was twelve feet deep in the main street, houses with people in them were taken off their foundations and carried out to sea.

The cattle-market land—one of the pieces the English farmers had brought into cultivation—was a complete wreck, the posts and rails from its fields were floating about the city. Instead of its own property it was covered with a miscellaneous collection of timber, barrels of salt fish, boats, dead horses, crosses from the Tintelef cemetery, part of a coffin, and most melancholy of all, a number of dead bodies, amongst them a woman with a child under each arm that she had tried, in vain, to save. The water was breaking against the cattle-market house, Stepan said, like the sea at the Cronstadt pier. All communication with the city, except by boat, was cut off ; it was surrounded by a lake some versts in width. A verst, we have been told, is about two thirds of a mile, scarcely differing from a kilometre. The water continued to rise until three p.m., when the wind changed to the north-west, and although the violence continued, the change of direction prevented the waves from rising any higher. Buildings of only one story were of course already filled, and the frightened occupants obliged to take refuge on the roofs, to save life as long as they were able.

In the afternoon, Daniel Wheeler says, they made an attempt to go towards the city, but found it unsafe to try further than the bank of the canal already mentioned. " The land under our care between this and the city was nearly all under water, so that we could hear nothing that night of the distress that prevailed there." There were two little households in the city about which they were specially anxious for intelligence—but they could only sit still and do nothing.

An Englishman, a Minister of the Society of Friends, had arrived a couple of months previously with the prospect of remaining the winter in Petersburg, an addition to the little "meeting" there which was hailed by the resident members with the greatest pleasure. Thomas Shillitoe and they were personally unknown to each other when they met, thus far from home, but Daniel Wheeler was soon able to write to one of his correspondents, "Thomas Shillitoe seems very comfortable amongst us," adding, "the more we know him the more we love him." He had a room in the house of an English family in the city—they could only spare him one, —but how it was situated with regard to this deluge, our friends could not tell. It was therefore a great relief to them when they saw him walking down the Moscow Road, on the following "First-day."

morning. The preceding day the road from the city had been quite impassable. We may venture to say that their meeting that morning was a truly solemn one.

From the windows of the house in which Thomas Shillitoe lodged he had a view down four streets, so that he was able to describe to his friends, later, what he had himself seen or personally experienced. It was probably much the same narrative as we find in his journal. He set out to take his usual walk but found to his surprise that the city was so surrounded by water he was obliged to return. Observing the servant of the house unable to reach home on her return from marketing, he says, "I went to inform her mistress of her situation and crossed the yard dry-shod; although not five minutes had elapsed before I attempted to make my way back, everything in the yard was floating. I stepped on a cellar window, and from that into the door of a bake-house, where the water followed me in such a body that I concluded I had no time to lose. I waded through it, and had I not done so promptly the rise of the water was so rapid I could not have reached the house.

"A hole was afterwards obliged to be cut in the wall of the bake-house to save the life of a woman who had taken shelter there. After getting quit of my wet clothes I took my stand at the windows of my sitting-room. The streets soon exhibited a scene of great distress, men wading up to their arm-pits in water, one woman up to her neck; horses and carriages swimming in the streets as long as it was possible to do so, the water in a short time rising to eight, then to twelve feet. The ground-floor of the house in which I was a resident was occupied by a grocer ; the water rose up to the ceiling of his shop and other apartments, without allowing him time to remove his goods or household stuff, its progress was so sudden and rapid. It was to be seen hastening up the sides of the houses, first touching the window-sill, then one pane of glass after another, until doors and windows were quite out of sight. Before noon the flood was so high no further effort towards safety was possible, and from that time until four in the afternoon the most awful stillness I ever witnessed prevailed. As far as my eyes could see not a person was visible at any window, nor anything that had life in the streets, except one poor horse that was fastened to a small cart, and had made his way so far towards home, but dared not venture further. He had preserved his life by placing his fore-feet on some steps which lay high above the footpaths, and was still barely able to keep his mouth above the water. About four p.m. a policeman came in a boat and set the poor prisoner free, when he quickly swam away. This policeman was the first person we had seen for the last five or six hours, excepting those living in the house. At four o'clock the flood began to retreat. Then came over the darkness of the night, which was complete in the streets, from the impossibility of lighting the lamps, adding greatly to the general difficulties and distress."

The heart-rending scenes made manifest by the next morning's light came to our friends' knowledge later, by degrees as one person after another brought intelligence from various parts of the city. But so far—that is at the time of Thomas Shillitoe's departure for home—no news had reached them from the second household that has been alluded to. Its peculiar difficulties will be better understood after a few words of explanation.

In the year 1820 Sheffield had sent yet a third representative to help the Emperor in his plans. A young woman Friend—Sarah Kilham, daughter of Alexander and Hannah Kilham—had gone over to Petersburg to conduct a " Lancasterian " boarding and day school there at the Emperor's request. The school prospered in her hands, she had a few boarders but more day-scholars, and they were all with her when the waters rose so suddenly. It was impossible to send them home and she was obliged to keep them for several days, which brought her into a state of embarrassment in the commissariat department. There was no chance of help from without, nor of letting the parents know of the safety of their children, she could only do her best for them, " trusting at the same time in the care of Him who could measure the waters in the hollow of His hand."

Sarah Kilham was a practical woman, and at once sent all the children to the upper story, while she waded for nearly an hour in the lower rooms, saving all she could lay her hands on, especially collecting food of all kinds and placing it on the highest level within her power. Happily she had a store of flour in the house, though no large quantity of anything except flour ; this she reserved until the bread had all vanished, and was thankful to have it in reserve,

as at that time bread could not be bought, the bakers'
ovens being still unusable from the effects of the
deluge. Her nice hot cakes were delightful to the
hungry children. The supply lasted until the flood
had so far abated that her friends could reach her.
By Monday, the tenth, Daniel Wheeler was able to
visit her, and to help in returning her charges to their
various families not any worse for their imprisonment
—not even a cold—but with a wonderful addition to
the experience of their short lives.

Their caretaker herself was the greatest sufferer in
that particular, but her chief thought seemed to be
what could she do for the still poorer households
around her. In our treasured bundle of old letters
there is a little note from her to the mistress of the
Okta farm, which Daniel Wheeler had evidently
taken charge of and forwarded to its destination. It was
written in the midst of her baking and fire-mending,
and was cheery as regards themselves, but the real
burden of it seems to be, " I do not know what to do
to help the poor around us." The needs of the little
ones everywhere were so overwhelming.

We do not know how far Sarah Kilham adhered to
the " Lancasterian system " in her schools, but it is
clear that she possessed the genuine self-forgetting
love for children which led to its original use. It was
a beautiful characteristic, belonging both to Joseph
Lancaster and to his contemporary, Heinrich Pesta-
lozzi, the Swiss educator he so much resembled.
Unfortunately we are compelled to add in both cases,
"until they were spoiled by public notice."

On the eleventh Daniel Wheeler writes, " I have
been both to-day and yesterday in the city, and have

heard such accounts of accumulated suffering as are impossible to be set forth. I fear the number of lives lost will amount to ten thousand, and the loss of cattle and property is immense. Whole squadrons of cavalry horses were drowned in their stables, and many others were only saved from a similar fate by being led upstairs. One Englishman, a horse-dealer, has lost all his horses."

General D'junkovski, the representative of the government with whom the English farmers transacted all their business, lost the whole of his winter provisions, both for his family and horses. The water rose almost to the second story in his house. His horses swam out of the stables, and, the yard gates being open, they got clear away, but were found all together on a piece of high ground a long way out.

It was pleasant to hear that when the water began to rise above its usual height in time of flood, the Emperor went in person and ordered the sentinels away from their different posts. When the palace became surrounded by water many feet deep, he appeared with the Empress on the balcony, encouraging the people to exertion, and offering rewards to those who would endeavour to save life, wherever he saw any particular danger ; by this, many were saved who would otherwise have been inevitably lost. " A subscription has been begun to-day for the benefit of the sufferers, to which the Emperor has contributed 1,000,000 roubles (£40,000 sterling), and he has ordered the military Governor to take care that the poor people are furnished with food."

As Thomas Shillitoe lived in the city and took a constitutional each morning, he saw many changes and incidents that escaped the notice of occasional visitors. "In my rambles this morning," he writes on one occasion, "it was distressing to observe the devastation that had taken place, for, as the water retired, it set wide open the doors of those shops which opened out into the streets, and the floatable articles were carried down to the canals and so out to sea. It was affecting, too, to watch the sorrowful countenances of the shop-keepers, as they stood at their doors whilst their servants were bringing out the remains of the wreck of their property. Some looked in awe-struck amazement, others as if paralysed, with no power left to lend a helping hand. Scarcely a word was heard in passing along." Three villages on the Peterhoff road were wholly swept away, men, women and children, cattle and horses all gone.

On the Catherine-hoff road, in a row of cottages, between two and three hundred women and children were found to have fallen victims to this awful visitation ; the men being from home, at work, escaped. If personal safety and mere life were everything worth living for, this might be called a happy escape, but we shall scarcely be surprised to learn that many of the poor men did not so consider it. When they learned that their families had all perished in their dwellings, or in some cases that houses and families had been carried out to sea, many of them became wildly mad, while others put an end to their earthly existence. What was life to them after such a loss ?

Another day Thomas Shillitoe notices the immense number of dead horses, cows and pigs that were being carted out of the city in order to be burned.

It was not considered wise to bury them lest the wolves should be attracted thereby.

Notwithstanding this awful visitation and the distress consequent upon it, the day after it happened the Commandant of the city ordered all the theatres to be opened in the evening, to " keep up the spirits of the people," but when the Emperor heard of it he countermanded the order. We hear that he proved himself to be, on this occasion, what it was the custom to call him—the " father of his people." He did not leave the wants of such of his poor subjects as had suffered from the inundation to the inspection of the police or any other of his officers, but went in person inquiring about and attending to them. Many of the survivors were, no doubt, in better condition as to outward comforts than they had been before—but alas ! he could not bring back their dead.

X.

A FOURTH TYPE OF QUAKER MINISTER.

THOMAS SHILLITOE, the English Friend who has already been spoken of as intending to spend the winter in Petersburg, and whose account of the Great Inundation—as he saw it—was laid under contribution in the last chapter, was still in Petersburg. He was a " Quaker Minister," and he was waiting for orders. A feeling that his Divine Master had work for him to do in that city had been present with him almost from his first arrival, but latterly the general sense that some kind of religious service would be required from him had been exchanged for the definite command to pay a visit to the Emperor.

By nature Thomas Shillitoe was a painfully nervous man ; so much so that to obey what he believed to be his Heavenly Father's orders, often called for an amount of physical as well as moral courage quite inconceivable to minds differently constituted. Moreover, he must often have endured a species of martyrdom in dreading difficulties which after all never became realities. His fear of falling into the hands of the Russian police was one of these trials. Also at this time there was added to the other perplexities troubling him, the practical question of the right method for making his desire known to the august monarch. He was a perfect stranger in the city, having felt it his duty, even in walking along the streets, to keep aloof from all companionship. Daniel Wheeler was but a recent acquaintance, and Thomas Shillitoe did not think it right to ask his help, for if anything went wrong with himself he might be involving in his own trouble a man who had been already so good a friend to him. Samuel Stansfield had permanently returned to England just before the storm burst that brought the late deluge to their doors, and the only other individual who knew of his present difficulty, and had, in fact, promised to help him, had drawn back from his promise in the end.

How *was* he to enter into communication with the Emperor in the first instance ? We cannot answer the question better than in the words of his own journal. He writes, " I therefore concluded it would be best for me to adopt my usual plan of doing my business myself, by addressing a note to the Secretary, leaving the result to that Almighty Power, who, I firmly believed, was able to make the way easy for me if it was his design I should be admitted to the Emperor."

The note was expressed as follows : " I am one of the Society of Friends ; and feeling, as I have done for some time, my mind exercised with apprehensions of religious duty, if possible to obtain an interview with the Emperor, I shall feel myself obliged to thee, his secretary, and served, by thy endeavouring to make such way for me as may be in thy power." No signature is appended in the journal.

The " Secretary," Prince Alexander Galitzin, otherwise known as the Emperor's Prime Minister, was
just the man to whom such a note would appeal.
He was a habitual reader of the Scriptures, and
more than that he was a practically religious man,
having been permitted to realise the meaning of
" quiet communion with his God," as our friends
Allen and Grellet have testified. It had been his
privilege from childhood to share the studies of the
Prince who was now at the head of the Empire, and
to whom he had ever been a loyal servant and a
faithful friend and adviser.

There could be no two opinions as to what the
Emperor's reception of the note would be. It was
so exactly in accordance with the wish he had expressed ten years before in London, that he must
have felt pleased by the writer's manner of approaching him. The accord was accidental and all the
more encouraging on that account. There was a
little delay in fixing a date for the interview, but only
because of the scarcity of leisure hours in the Emperor's life. He was quite unacquainted with Thomas
Shillitoe, but his remembrance of William Allen and
Stephen Grellet was as warm and affectionate as ever,
and he was quite ready to welcome another messenger bearing similar credentials.

An inquiry after the welfare of these Friends
opened the way for a very free exchange of senti-
ments, and Alexander soon learned to appreciate the
new envoy for the simple-hearted transparency of his
personal character, at once adding him to the number
of his valued friends. As he shook hands with his
visitor at the close of the interview, he said, " I shall

not consider this a parting opportunity, Mr. Shillitoe, but shall expect another visit from you before you set off for your own home." This was a great relief to our timid friend, who was feeling he had not yet expressed all that was given him to say.

A second interview was arranged early in the New Year, and in the pages of his journal he has left a long account of it, and of the Emperor's remarkably clear and candid acknowledgment of the valuable help his acquaintance with the " Quakers " and their principles had been to him. It is only natural that members of that Society should feel gratified by such an acknowledgment, but we must not lose sight of the fact that unless Alexander had come to England in a receptive state of mind, and seeking for help, what he heard and saw there would have been merely a dead language to him. But the marvel is that such a softened, seeking heart was to be found in the person of Alexander, the son of the Emperor Paul, and the grandson of the Empress Catharine !

The thought is suggested that probably the companionship in study, which, commenced in youth, continued through life between the two Alexanders, and which is spoken of as a great privilege for the Prince Galitzin, had proved no less a privilege for the future Emperor, in helping to counteract the less desirable influence of at least two of his ancestors. At any rate, whatever the instruments employed in his training, the Emperor, who sat talking confidentially to Thomas Shillitoe, was a ruler to be thankful for. The two men parted with mutual respect and affection, and Thomas Shillitoe felt once more that he had accomplished all that was at present required of him, and was now at liberty to return to England.

We find in a letter from George Edmondson to his sister at the end of that inundation year, the following words, " A report has got abroad, we understand, that you may shortly expect us home again. Although we cannot deny that there is a great alteration here in the state of things, nothing has occurred to lead us to suppose that we shall be disturbed. . . . Our own liberty of action is untouched, and, except that we see less of the Emperor, no difference is perceptible so far as we are concerned."

They found it needful to be very cautious about the wording of their letters at this time. It was within the last year of Alexander's life—he was not strong and many of those about him were suspicious and jealous. Still there was evidently no danger of our English Friends being disturbed by the Russian government in the work they were carrying on with so much advantage to the country.

Yet, after all, the young couple whose fortunes for the last six or seven years, have been followed, we hope, with kindly interest, *did* return to England in the following year—1825. Personal considerations alone led to the move. The winter that had already begun when George wrote that letter to his sister proved a very trying one to his wife, and it was decided that they must return permanently to their native land.

Daniel Wheeler acknowledged the difference that the absence of his lieutenant would make to him, but health so unmistakably demanded the change that he could not object to it. He therefore acquiesced in the decision, leaving his own future movements to the disposing of the same Power that he believed had sent him to Petersburg at first, and had also provided him, thus far, with the needed assistance. There was still one large tract of land to cultivate, and he determined, if possible, to finish the work he had begun. He had been a soldier before he became a Friend, and he retained the soldier's instinct of obedience to the orders of his commanding officer. When he left the army in consequence of his altered views, he did not lay aside this habit of obeying, but he looked to a different source for his orders. It was to a Heavenly Commander that he now turned for directions as to his movements, and when received, they were as implicitly followed in his daily life as ever command by word of mouth had been obeyed when he was a young man in the ranks.

The piece of marsh land still uncultivated was known as Shoosharry, according to Daniel Wheeler's spelling; Shushari we have seen it given by more recent travellers. It was the largest plot of the whole, and eventually turned out to be the best land. It was at a greater distance from the city than any previously under their care. At the time Daniel Wheeler decided to undertake it, the house he and his family were to inhabit was in the heart of a wood near this great bog—a most unhealthy situation. But the whole family were of one mind; they believed it was required of them to finish their work—to go to Shoosharry—and they went, prepared to accept the consequences whatever they might prove to be.

For several reasons, amongst others his own somewhat failing health, it was desirable that Daniel

Wheeler should pay a visit to England while George could still be left in charge of the land. The way was made easy for him to do so by an inquiry from the Emperor as to " Mr. Wheeler's state of health." His royal friend knew that during the long absence of half his family in England in 1823-4, Daniel Wheeler had himself been visited by a serious and dangerous illness, which at one time the patient thought would prevent their ever meeting again on earth. He was careful to keep the knowledge of it from the absent ones, as the time of year was not favourable for their return to him. But some strong impulse sent them home before they were expected.

The sound of wheels was heard suddenly one evening at the end of May, 1824, and almost before the father and two sons had time to wonder who their visitors could be, the whole party were in the house and once more a united family. The long trial of faith and patience was soon forgotten in the joy of their return.

The Emperor did not seem to have forgotten however, and the individual of whom his kind inquiries were made suggesting that a change would be a great advantage to Daniel Wheeler, an official intimation was promptly forwarded to him that he was at liberty to proceed to England *on a visit* whenever he pleased to go. Thus way was open for him to accompany his friend Thomas Shillitoe on his return home in the spring of 1825, or rather we may say Thomas Shillitoe accompanied *him*, for he speaks with thankfulness of the prospect of such a caretaker. They travelled over-land through Prussia, a cold rough journey, lasting six and thirty days. This curtailed the visitor's time in England very considerably, allowing him only three months to spend amongst his friends and relatives.

In the autumn of that same year, shortly after Daniel Wheeler's return to Russia, arrangements were finally made to set the young couple at liberty. Robert Worthy, one of the farmers who had gone out with the party in 1818, and who had developed into a trusted, confidential helper, was to take charge at Okta, and other duties were to be distributed amongst the younger members of Daniel Wheeler's own family.

The sister who accompanied them from England had gone home the year before. She was the first to show signs of failing strength, and finding that Captain Wharton, of whose kindness during their voyage out the trio retained such pleasant recollections, was on the point of sailing again for England, the decision was hastily arrived at that she should avail herself of his escort.

u t there was still a trio to take a passage for in 1825. There was a two-year-old little maiden to be introduced to her expectant grandparents. She was the childish lover of the pictures which were then but newly purchased, and she is trying to-day to re-tell the stories heard from one person and another, so many years ago. To a few readers some of them may prove twice-told-tales, for certain of them have appeared in print, but as this was in 1879, she hopes they will still be found interesting.

The party sailed in the *Little Alster*, as Daniel Wheeler calls the vessel, at the end of September or the beginning of October.

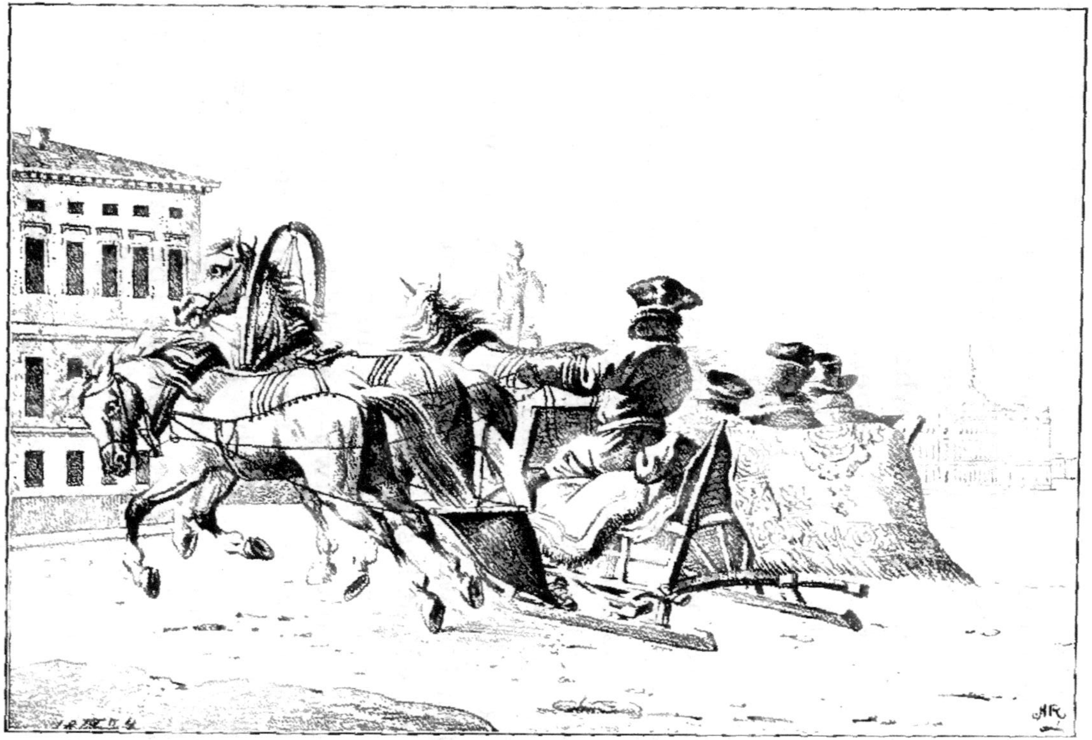

LARGE PRIVATE SLEDGE.

Thus terminated George Edmondson's seven years' connection with the work in Russia—his personal connection that is—it was not possible for him to lose interest in it, and a letter now and then from his former " captain " kept him acquainted for the next few years with any important changes. His own future was left with perfect confidence to Divine guidance. He would have to begin life entirely anew in England. He had left it at an early age, before the end of his apprenticeship, we may remember, and now that he was returning thither he knew neither where his lot might be cast, nor which of his late occupations he should pursue. He had been both teacher and farmer, and he would follow either life as way opened. His inclination perhaps leaned towards the former, yet in any case he felt the seven years just passed were not likely to be thrown away. But the further record of his life cannot be said to belong to " Quaker Pioneers in Russia."

Yet, even as we write, an incident occurs to us which it may be well to mention here, although it was a quarter of a century later that the curious little meeting we are thinking of took place. At that time George Edmondson was Principal of Queenwood College in Hampshire, and returning from London one afternoon, he entered a carriage at Waterloo Station, in which a gentleman and lady were already seated. Scarcely had the train begun to move when his ear caught sounds to which it had long been a stranger. His companions were conversing in Russ. So long as their chat was on unimportant subjects he kept silence, but when family matters were introduced he thought it time to say a word himself. Forty or

fifty years ago the knowledge of the Russian language
was not common in England, and they would feel
quite safe in using it, safer indeed, than if they had
spoken in either French or German.

" It is right to let you know that you are understood, my friends," George Edmondson remarked
in Russ, to the great surprise of his fellow travellers ;
and naturally much inquiry followed. They were
a gentleman and his daughter travelling in this
country, and were highly delighted to hear thus
unexpectedly the familiar words of their own
language.

" Had the gentleman been lately in St. Petersburg ? "

" Not lately, many years ago," he answered.

" Ah ! then you should visit it again. You have
no idea of the improvement that has been made all
round the city. The Emperor Alexander began a
great work. He determined to drain the marshy
land which came, as you may remember, very close to
the city gates, and now I can scarcely describe to
you the wonderful transformation."

" It is not necessary," he replied quietly, " These
hands helped to make the first drains." Upon which
the surprise of his travelling companions was greater
still.

Of course he then had to explain his connection
with the work, and to describe the state in which
they found the land. But when the Russian gentleman took up the thread of the narrative, and drew
pictures of the luxuriance and beauty of the same
localities at the time he left the city, George
Edmondson was obliged to confess that without the

testimony of an eye-witness he could not have imagined so splendid a result. With mutual interest and pleasure they compared notes about the past and present, but amongst their numerous questions, they unfortunately forgot to ask each other's name and destination.

They must have been talking a couple of hours, when they were interrupted by the porter's cry of "Bishopstoke Junction! All change at Bishopstoke!" The carriage door was thrown open, they all instinctively alighted, still talking earnestly, but still forgetting to inquire if their roads continued in the same direction. Evidently they did not. The fellow-passengers were separated in the crowd and this strangely interesting encounter came suddenly to an end.

It would be useless to attempt a description of George Edmondson's feelings of disappointment and annoyance with himself as he travelled on to Dunbridge. There was nothing to be done, however, the fellow-travellers never met again! And we are obliged to confess that the only apparent result of their coming together, was a stranger's disinterested testimony to the material success of Daniel Wheeler's work. What has been its deeper effect is beyond our ken; but our faith is strong that in the Spiritual world too, such efforts are never allowed to die.

> "Tho' *men* may die and be forgot,
> Work done for *God*, it dieth not."

XI.

SHOOSHARRY.

THE first communication received from Peters
burg, after the young couple returned to
England, conveyed sad news—the death
of the deeply lamented and justly beloved Emperor,
which occurred in December, 1825. It came as a
great shock to his English friends, especially to those
who had been recipients of his kind thought and
consideration. His age was only forty-three, and
though far from strong, the state of his health had not
been the cause of alarm.

The Empress Elizabeth was the patient who
occasioned the greatest anxiety to Dr. Wylie, their
English physician, and it was on her account that
Taganrog, in the Crimea, was chosen as the residence
of the Royal couple that winter. The Empress did
not wish to be separated from her husband, and he
chose a place which he could make his head-quarters
in the neighbourhood of the army, and which was,
at the same time, a suitable locality for the invalid.
"The climate immediately surrounding Taganrog is
considered very healthy," Daniel Wheeler says, "but
at only a short distance from it the neighbourhood
has a character quite the reverse ; and it seems that
Alexander had been beyond the healthy boundary,

and had taken cold on the South coast. . . . I
believe it has been the lot of few monarchs to end
their days, whilst in the meridian of power, in a retreat
so quiet and so distant from all the pageantry of the
court. He may be said to have died in the bosom of
his family." This was a truly welcome expression of
opinion from a man so cautious as to the words he
used as our friend Daniel Wheeler, and so capable
of forming an unbiassed judgment, for suspicions were
rife in several quarters.

The Empress only survived her husband five
months. There was, at first, a time of uncertainty in
the country with regard to the succession. Constantine, the brother next in age to Alexander, did not
possess the qualities required for a good Emperor of
"All the Russias," a fact of which he was himself
humbly conscious. He had been accustomed to rely
upon his elder brother's guidance in his decisions and
actions, and now, having lost his guide, he shrank
from accepting the responsibility of the crown. There
were those about the court, however, who insisted on
the legitimate order of succession.

Alexander's death took place in the far south of
the empire, we may remember, at a great distance
from the capital in time as well as in measured miles ;
for only a quarter of the wonderful century had been
lived through, which, before its close, had done so
much towards " annihilating time and space." The
delay thus occasioned in communicating arrangements
between Taganrog and Petersburg gave this party an
opportunity of proclaiming Constantine, and the
army was required to take the oath of allegiance to
him.

We will not impute motives to those who preferred the weaker governor, but may rejoice that the struggle which ensued within the next few days, ended in the ultimate choice of the younger and stronger brother —Nicholas. There was some bewilderment in the minds of the soldiers when they were called upon to swear fealty to Nicholas only ten days after they had taken the same oath to Constantine, and the army was divided in its opinion, for it was natural to them to suspect some kind of foul play. But the appearance of the two brothers riding side by side in the streets of Moscow allayed the fears of the troops in that respect ; the cordiality and real brotherly love between them were unmistakeable. Moreover, Nicholas announced that he intended to govern as Alexander had done, and everything quickly settled down again. Such was the aspect of this brief rebellion, which the present writer had laid before her when she was ready for that page of history.

These upheavals had no effect upon our friends at the various farms however. They became as familiar with the presence in the neighbourhood of the sword-bearing branch of the army as they had hitherto been with the appearance of the wielders of the spade. They found the two divisions equally inoffensive so far as they themselves were concerned. Once only they received a visit from a large party of them, but they were not entirely unprepared and were able to entertain them in true Quaker fashion. Daniel Wheeler's old experience led him to the conclusion, from the appearance of the men he saw about, that they were weary, cold and famished, and he warned his family that they might probably be called upon to find provisions for them. About one o'clock, a colonel, four other officers, and seventy hussars entered their premises, and without hesitation, men and horses were all fed.

" It is well they came to us," Daniel Wheeler writes in his journal, " as there was no other house in their whole range that could have provided food for both men and horses. The whole party were very civil and very thankful, but they had not been with us two hours, when the appearance of a Cossack riding in haste along the high road caused their speedy departure."

Two letters from Daniel Wheeler still remain unnoticed. The earlier one, written in 1826, has always been looked upon by us as a marvellous specimen of letter-writing—quite worthy of a glass case in a museum, for the power and inclination to produce such a piece of work are certainly lost to this generation. It is written on the usual large foolscap paper, and no room is wasted on margins. Indeed, the only unused spaces on the whole sheet are those left vacant for the seal and the address. The lines are close—not more than a third of an inch apart, and the crossing, which is done with beautiful regularity, measures even more lines to the inch than that. Someone had the curiosity to measure with a work-box tape.

The whole appearance of the letter confirms the assurance given on the first page, that the writer is in very good health—stronger and better, he says, than when he first stepped on Russian soil. This he mentions with a note of thankfulness for his increased vigour, " not having had a superabundance of hands

lately to overlook the now very widely extended work."
His son William attends to the accounts, Daniel
Wheeler says, as he understands Russ perfectly, and
Charles superintends at Volkovo and the Cattle-market
lands. Daniel Wheeler himself spends a large pro-
portion of each week at Shoosharry, accompanied by
his daughters, and is evidently appreciating its
capabilities more and more highly as one improvement after another becomes an accomplished fact.

The front of the house had been raised, and a
shrubbery planted, and two winding roads were in
process of construction, one macadamised the other
paved with stone, which gave the feeling of a better
chance of communication with their fellow-creatures
than seemed possible when they first visited the new
home.

Immense fires appear to have been the peculiar
feature of that summer—a long hot one. The writer
of the letter gives a formidable list of localities where
the woods had been entirely destroyed, names no
doubt well known to his correspondent but conveying
to us only the general idea of a vast extent of flame
and damage. He speaks of fifty versts being
alight in one line, and the growing grass burning like
paper. The scarcity of water on the Shoosharry land,
added greatly to the difficulty of subduing the terrible
enemy.

The damp clay, of which there was a depth of
several feet under the fine black soil on the surface,
was their chief resource, and indeed it was the best
check they could have for a fire that had once taken
a firm hold. The house and very extensive outbuildings were all built of wood, and of course were in

peculiar danger. These were surrounded by a broad zone of clay which had been carefully cleared of everything inflammable, and even then it was only by constant watchfulness that the buildings were saved.

A pond was quickly dug, and some of the drains were turned into it, which supplied a thick, black sort of water better than nothing, they thought, in the battle with the destroying element, but they found the men were glad to drink it, and it did not seem to do them any harm. Then a second pond was added, and a large bath for the use of the men, which was lined with some of the clay displaced in the digging. For the use of the house a third pond was prepared, filled from their large extent of roofing, so that only rain and snow were the sources of its supply, filtered afterwards to the best of their ability.

Here the writer checks himself—confessing that he could fill his sheet with nothing but a history of the land, for "Shoosharry will be, in the end, the nicest situation in the neighbourhood of Petersburg."

But the family were then still living at the house on the Moscow Road, and before closing his letter he says he must tell of a little adventure they had there a few weeks previously. They had been troubled by persons prowling about the premises at night and trying to get into the yard. He often had large sums of Government money in the house and, no doubt, this was known.

"As we could not resort to force," he wrote, "yet it was needful something should be done; it was concluded best to endeavour to take some of the offenders into custody by having our own people in ambush. One night when someone was trying to force open the gate next the lane, our men being ready at their post, the fastenings were imperceptibly loosened, and the enemy permitted to enter the garrison, when he was immediately surrounded and taken prisoner without the least violence on either part. He had a large stake in his hand, but he was so taken by surprise he seemed bereft of power to use it, and tamely submitted to be bound and locked up until day-light with two of our men over him as sentinels. He proved to be a soldier of the Proloffsky regiment, and was accordingly escorted next day, bound hand and foot, to his officer. His accomplices had remained about the house more than two hours expecting a signal as soon as their leader had got possession and despatched our watchman. All had been done so quietly they had no idea what had become of their hero."

The premises were visited even after that in the long dark nights, therefore, it was thought wiser to decline for the future to receive any store of the Government money, so as to remove the chief temptation.

The only remaining letter in Daniel Wheeler's division of the packet we have been looking over, bears date Shoosharry, 1831. He and Jane Wheeler had together paid a visit to England in 1830-31, which was found desirable on account of the latter's health. It seems that circumstances, sometimes on one side sometimes on the other, had combined to prevent a meeting between the two men whom we may still call Captain and Lieutenant, and the letter begins with an echo of George Edmondson's disappointment at the lost opportunity. In fact a melancholy tone pervades the whole. The writer says, "The prospect of returning again to this country after the London Yearly Meeting, was tinged with a gloom which before we never witnessed, owing to the dreadful struggle between it and Poland on one hand, and the awful visitation of cholera on the other." But he can still say that evidence has been again and again vouchsafed that he is in his "proper allotment."

"The morning we reached Cronstadt," the letter continues, "115 died, and in the city the deaths amounted to 800 per diem, ... yet, still more terrifying than the ravages of the fatal disease, is the idea the people had got into their heads, that the mortality was occasioned by poison administered by Polish agents, and nothing for a time could equal the outrageous conduct of the rabble. The hospitals were attacked, the doctors killed, and the patients set at liberty.

"A man belonging to us was taken up in the street by the police; most likely he had had too much to drink; but they insisted that he had the cholera, and though he pleaded that he was quite well, they carried him off to a hospital. He was one of those who escaped from a window when the place was stormed by the mob. He gladly made his way back to us and has never been ill at all!"

They had more than five hundred men working for them on the land, and had no serious case of cholera amongst them. The brothers, who had been left in charge during their father's absence, had been constantly on the watch, and the slightest symptom of illness was promptly treated to the best of their ability.

At the British Consul's office all letters were taken in with a pair of tongs, they were told, for fear of infection ; our letter looks as if it had been received on the point of a sword, there is a cut more than an inch long through all its folds.

Just at the end of the epistle are a few lines descriptive of Shoosharry, as it appeared to their writer on his return thither ; and again it is evident that this last of their transformations was becoming a favourite home to him.

" This place is much altered," he tells George, " and is fast improving, as it is now the high road to Moscow. . . . We are building a new village not far from our house. . . . The land is very fruitful and the place generally healthy," and so on.

We heartily rejoice with our dear Friend at the success with which his efforts had been blest, and yet we cannot help feeling that his growing attachment for Shoosharry, as the place developed under his superintending care, must have added to the difficulty of tearing himself away when the Master's order came to him to leave it.

In the letter quoted above, Daniel Wheeler again mentions that the comforting assurance had been repeatedly vouchsafed to him that he was on his proper allotment, and we have reason to believe that the same feeling remained with him throughout the year 1831. But in 1832, when he had been fifteen years steadily engaged in what we have already spoken of as a " unique experiment," he became aware that a change in the service required of him was probable.

It appeared to be his duty to relinquish his engagement in Russia, and to look to returning to England ; not however with a view to settling down there ; although what place was to be his next "allotment" was not yet shown to him.

His faith was equal to the demand upon it, and he was able to say the same for the various members of his family circle—as yet unvisited by death. Step by step, as his future path was made plain to himself, he consulted them as to what he proposed to do, and in each case he found that his proposal, after resting in their minds, received their entire assent.

The Russian Government suggested, on the receipt of Daniel Wheeler's resignation of his position, that his eldest son should take his place, and that everything else should remain on its original footing. And as no light shone on his path further than England, his wife felt that, at present at least, it was her duty to remain in Russia. The buoyancy of spirit which distinguished Daniel Wheeler in the early days at Okta and Volkovo was, perhaps, subdued later under the weight of responsibility laid upon him, but there was neither hesitation nor looking back.

We noticed in an earlier chapter the fact that no public service seemed to be required of him in Russia ; now, on the contrary, after the work there was given up to his son William, his whole life seemed to be a series of public services ; first during his five years on the islands in the North and South Pacific, and later in some parts of North America.

We do not, however, propose to follow him on either journey, but practically, to take leave of him as he quits the country where he had been for so long a time the chief and most highly valued of the Pioneer Band.

His illness in England, his wife's death, his brief visit to his sorrowing children at Shoosharry, and the offer of his son Charles to accompany him on his long voyage, though most touching incidents well known to many Friends, do not strictly belong to Daniel Wheeler's life in Russia.

We have a few mementos from Tahiti, sent "with D.W.'s. love to G.E.," but no letter after the one already noticed.